9/kt

Marie-Louise von Franz, Honorary Patron

**Studies in Jungian Psychology
by Jungian Analysts**

Daryl Sharp, General Editor

MILES TO GO
BEFORE I SLEEP
Growing Up Puer

Another Jungian Romance

DARYL SHARP

For Bo Peep, me, Sophia, and extended family.

Note: Some material here originally appeared in my other works.
Thanks to Library of America for the Emerson passages.

Library and Archives Canada Cataloguing in Publication

Sharp, Daryl, 1936-
  Miles to go before I sleep : growing up puer : another Jungian
romance / Daryl Sharp.

(Studies in Jungian psychology by Jungian analysts ; 134)
Includes bibliographical references and index.

ISBN 978-1-894574-36-5

  1. Typology (Psychology) 2. Jungian psychology. I. Title.
II. Series: Studies in Jungian psychology by Jungian analysts 134.

BF698.3.S52 2012   155.2'644   C2012-902779-0

INNER CITY BOOKS
Box 1271, Station Q, Toronto, ON M4T 2P4, Canada.
Telephone (416) 927-0355 / Fax (416) 924-1814
Toll-free (Canada and U.S.): Tel. 1-888-927-0355 / Fax 1-888-924-1814
Web site: www.innercitybooks.net / E-mail: booksales@innercitybooks.net

Honorary Patron: Marie-Louise von Franz.
Publisher and General Editor: Daryl Sharp.
Associate Editor: Frith Luton.
Senior Editor: Victoria B. Cowan.
Office Manager: Scott Milligen.

INNER CITY BOOKS was founded in 1980 to promote the
understanding and practical application of the work of C. G. Jung.

Cover: Stone scribe on cornice of Chartres Cathedral (17th century).

Printed and bound in Canada by Thistle Printing Limited.

CONTENTS

*See final pages for other Inner City titles
and how to order them*

Stopping by Woods on a Snowy Evening

Whose woods these are I think I know.
His house is in the village though;
He will not see me stopping here
To watch his woods fill up with snow.

My little horse must think it queer
To stop without a farmhouse near
Between the woods and frozen lake
The darkest evening of the year.

He gives his harness bells a shake
To ask if there is some mistake.
The only other sound's the sweep
Of easy wind and downy flake.

The woods are lovely, dark and deep.
But I have promises to keep,
And miles to go before I sleep,
And miles to go before I sleep.[1]

[1] Robert Frost, in "The Poetry of Robert Frost," Ed. Edward Connery Lathem, from *The Random House Book of Poetry for Children*. (See Frost reading it on YouTube)

PREFACE

Two of my esteemed Jungian colleagues, Mario Jacoby and James Hillman, died this year (2011). I am now one of the few surviving second-tier Jungian acolytes who endeavor to keep Jung's message alive in our hectic extraverted collective culture, where ambition and electronic toys are valued more than character development. I despair that Jung's ideas will ever crack the mainstream, though I am heartened to see several videos of him explaining his views on YouTube.

And so I wonder, after writing twenty books, what more do I have to say? This is the question that keeps me awake night and day.

I was recently alerted to my mortality by a week's stay in hospital. I was experiencing extreme fatigue and difficulty breathing. My doctor sent me to emergency where my symptoms were immediately recognized as CHF (congestive heart failure). They put me on oxygen for a week and an intravenous diuretic to drain the fluids from my lungs and heart. I was x-rayed, MRI'd, echocardiogrammed and ultrasounded. They took my blood pressure every twenty minutes, drew blood from my arms three times a day, and constantly monitored my vital organs with space-age body patches. Every day they asked me if I knew who and where I was.

I didn't mind the inactivity and incarceration; it was in fact a welcome holiday away from my lonely turret and business concerns. I enjoyed the attention and Razr flirted outrageously with the nurses. Of course, I had to cancel my planned Christmas vacation at a semi-nude Jamaican resort (Hedonism II), but what the hell. Every twelve-hour change in shift brought a new nurse more lovely than the last—East Indian, Pakistani, Thai, Israeli, Russian, Korean, Samoan and more. They did everything to make me feel comfortable but hop into bed with me. Never mind, I was catheterized and wasn't up to much except trying to sleep between tests. There was nothing to complain about except the food. However hard they try—and I think they do—every hospital serves unpalatable gruel. The soup is generally good, also the fruit. It's hard to kill a banana.

But seriously, it finally got me thinking. What am I here for?

This new "Jungian romance" may or may not be an answer.

INTRODUCTION

I will begin this book with the classic song written by Hoagy Carmichael in 1934 (put to music by Johnny Mercer), and see where that leads:

Skylark
Have you anything to say to me?
Won't you tell me where my love can be?
Is there a meadow in the mist
Where someone's waiting to be kissed?

Oh skylark
Have you seen a valley green with spring?
Where my heart can go a journeying
Over the shadows and the rain
To a blossom covered lane

And in your lonely flight
Haven't you heard the music in the night?
Wonderful music
Faint as a will o' the wisp
Crazy as a loon
Sad as a gypsy serenading the moon

Oh skylark
I don't know if you can find these things
But my heart is riding on your wings
So if you see them anywhere
Won't you lead me there
Oh skylark
Won't you lead me there?[2]

I imagine that this song can serve as the leitmotif of the puer aeternus: the adolescent longing for a loved one forever out of reach. In middle age he is still riding on her wings and can become "crazy as a loon" and "sad as a gypsy" without a paramour. This is my current fate, although I fudge

---

[2] Performed by many singers over the years since 1928; Ascap.

it with active imaginations and a crush on a Little Bo Peep in Switzerland. She won me over via the video of Bonnie Tyler singing "Total Eclipse of the Heart,"[3] which blew me away. I am a Romantic, after all, responsive and vulnerable to the love of women. Here are the lyrics:

> Turn around, every now and then
> I get a little bit lonely and you're never coming round
> Turn around, every now and then
> I get a little bit tired of listening to the sound of my tears
>
> Turn around, every now and then
> I get a little bit nervous that the best of all the years have gone by
> Turn around, every now and then
> I get a little bit terrified and then I see the look in your eyes
>
> Turn around, bright eyes
> Every now and then I fall apart
> Turn around, bright eyes
> Every now and then I fall apart
>
> Turnaround, every now and then
> I get a little bit restless and I dream of something wild
> Turnaround, every now and then
> I get a little bit helpless and I'm lying like a child in your arms
>
> Turn around, every now and then
> I get a little bit angry and I know I've got to get out and cry
> Turnaround, every now and then
> I get a little bit terrified but then I see the look in your eyes
>
> Turn around bright eyes
> Every now and then I fall apart
> Turn around bright eyes
> Every now and then I fall apart
>
> And I need you now tonight
> And I need you more than ever
> And if you only hold me tight
> We'll be holding on forever
>
> And we'll only be making it right
> 'Cause we'll never be wrong
>
> Together we can take it to the end of the line

---

[3] See her do it on YouTube.

Your love is like a shadow on me all of the time
I don't know what to do and I'm always in the dark
We're living in a powder keg and giving off sparks

I really need you tonight
Forever's gonna start tonight
Forever's gonna start tonight

Once upon a time I was falling in love
Now I'm only falling apart
There's nothing I can do
A total eclipse of the heart

Once upon a time there was light in my life
But now there's only love in the dark
Nothing I can say
A total eclipse of the heart

Turnaround, bright eyes
Turnaround, bright eyes

Turnaround, every now and then
I know you'll never be the boy you always wanted to be
Turnaround, every now and then
I know you'll always be the only boy who wanted me the way that I am

Turn around, every now and then
I know there's no one in the universe as magical and wondrous as you
Turnaround, every now and then
I know there's nothing any better, there's nothing that I just wouldn't do

Turn around bright eyes
Every now and then I fall apart
Turnaround bright eyes
Every now and then I fall apart

And I need you now tonight
And I need you more than ever
And if you'll only hold me tight
We'll be holding on forever

And we'll only be making it right
'Cause we'll never be wrong

. . . .

I really need you tonight
Forever's gonna start tonight
Forever's gonna start tonight

Once upon a time I was falling in love
Now I'm only falling apart
There's nothing I can do
A total eclipse of the heart

Once upon a time there was light in my life
But now there's only love in the dark
Nothing I can say
A total eclipse of the heart

A total eclipse of the heart
A total eclipse of the heart
Turn around, bright eyes
Turn around, bright eyes
Turn around.

Well, I could say more about my precious Bo Peep and how she came into my life, but I don't want to embarrass her, and she is, after all, just a metaphor for every woman a puer has ever loved. Of course the real woman is not a metaphor, but you get what I mean. It is true that I wish we were physically closer (and I am creating an ensuiteheart in my house to that end). But for now, it is enough to know that she is there and that we have strong feelings for each other. Now, I ask you, what else is important in life except to love and be loved in return, a sentiment popularized in song by Nat King Cole, his daughter Natalie, Frank Sinatra, Sarah Vaughan, and many, many others:

There was a boy
A very strange enchanted boy
They say he wandered very far, very far
Over land and sea
A little shy
And sad of eye
But very wise
Was he

And then one day,
A magic day he came my way
And while we spoke of many things, fools and kings
This he said to me
"The greatest thing
You'll ever learn

Is just to love
And be loved
In return."

"The greatest thing
You'll ever learn
Is just to love
And be loved
In return."[4]

The puer is a "nature boy," for sure, though he may not favor the out-of-doors, hiking or gardening. His nature is to be "natural," unfettered by collective mores. This is to some extent laudable, but it can get him into deep doo-doo.

The typical puer is impatient. He is brim-full of fantasies and wants to make things happen. But with experience he learns that he can't control the world. In love relationships he tends to get ahead of himself, anticipating the best, or the worst. He is not for black or white, but flounders in the gray. And *desire* is such a capricious handmaiden; it cannot be commanded, though once aroused may not be denied.

Come to that, think of the difference between "putative" and "presumptive." The former means supposed, reputed, alleged, assumed, while presumptive means probable, plausible, possible.

I hope that helps. But still, can I say, for instance, that Bo Peep is my putative paramour, or is presumptive more accurate? Up for grabs.

****

Incidentally, an African-American ragtime pianist named Reggie Duvalle gave the teen-aged Hoagy Carmichael a piece of advice: "Never play anything that ain't *right,*" he said. "You may not make a lot of money, but you'll never get hostile with yourself."[5]

That also sounds a lot like good Jungian advice to me......

---

[4] "Nature Boy," from *The Greatest of Nat King Cole,* words and music by Eden Ahbez; Ascap.
[5] Hoagland Carmichael, *The Stardust Road & Sometimes I Wonder: The Autobiographies of Hoagy Carmichael:* p. vi.

1
THE PUER AND ME

But I have gotten ahead of myself. The Robert Frost poem quoted here at the beginning more or less explains the title of this book—joyful living in the face of mortality (I hear sleep = die). Here I want to explore the subtitle—the history and psychology of the *puer aeternus* motif. This is not easy for me to summarize here, for it has been in my head and books for over forty years. However, I will try to square the circle.

For a start, the term is rooted in Greek mythology, a moniker ascribed to the ageless Greek gods, like Dionysus and Eros. The term *puer aeternus* itself comes from Ovid's *Metamorphoses*, where it is applied to the child-god Iacchus in the Eleusinian mysteries. He is the divine youth born in the night in the typical mother-cult mystery of Eleusis. He is a kind of redeemer, a god of vegetation and resurrection, the god of divine youth, corresponding to such gods as the oriental Tammuzi, and Attis and Adonis.

Such men never grow up, never leave the bosom of mother-love. They find it difficult to commit to another, and are vulnerable to a woman's seductive wiles. They are devoted to self-gratification; that is, they are essentially narcissistic and oriented to pleasure, often addicted.

Typically, the puer is romantic and chivalrous, keen to please women. He is hard working and loyal to an employer, though paradoxically he finds it difficult to get out of bed, for he feels safe under the covers and dreads facing the routine tasks ahead, however well he performs them.

Now, the late Marie-Louise von Franz (1915-1998), long-time associate of C. G. Jung and doyenne of Jungian analysts throughout her life, set the benchmark for understanding puer psychology in her ground-breaking study, *Puer Aeternus,* first published in 1970.[6] I do not try to

---

[6] I republished this in 2000 as *The Problem of the Puer Aeternus.* (Inner City Books, title no. 87 in Studies in Jungian Psychology by Jungian Analysts) I can also recommend Ann Yeoman, *Now or Neverland: Peter Pan and the Myth of Eternal Youth.*

outdo Dr. von Franz in this book. I may quote or paraphrase her at times in an attempt to explicate the syndrome, but all said, my writing is only a complement—or compliment—to her work. Note that women do not escape this appellation; given a similar syndrome, the puer's opposite number is called a puella. And need it be said that puers and puellas attract each other like moths to a flame? Well, that is a given—life as many of us know it.

Let's be clear right away, the puer syndrome is many faceted, as exemplified by most men I know, but perhaps the best place to begin to get a handle on the psychology of it is to start with von Franz's acute, succinct characterization:

> In general, the man who is identified with the archetype of the *puer aeternus* remains too long in adolescent psychology; that is, all those characteristics that are normal in a youth of seventeen or eighteen are continued into later life, coupled in most cases with too great a dependence on the mother.[7]

This apparent excoriation of the puer has driven many men to distraction, including myself. Some readers have even confessed to feeling suicidal after digesting her words. Personally, rather than jumping offa bridge, I went into analysis, which proved to be a salutary course for me, as I subsequently trained to become a Jungian analyst and then fortuitously founded Inner City Books. Lucky me, to find my calling at the age of forty-five. It is in fact generally the puer's fate to find himself in midlife or even later (though this is not to say that every late bloomer is of the puer clan, or that every puer is destined to bloom late).

Actually, the puer syndrome is not as bad as it might first sound, and much depends, of course, on one's typology. The puer/puella generally has the charm, enthusiasm and exuberance of youth, and is often creative and inclined to spiritual values. But more of that later.

****

Now, although I originally fell into the arms of rock 'n roll via the

---

[7] *The Problem of the Puer Aeternus,* p. 7. It is worth noting here that von Franz's puer comments are surrounded by an explication of St. Exupéry's novel, *The Little Prince.*

vibrant, incomparable lyrics, harmonics, and musical lilt of the Beatles,[8] I have lately been seduced anew by The Band, whose celebratory concert, THE LAST WALTZ (1976), featuring guests Neil Young, Bob Dylan, Van Morrison, Joni Mitchel, Neil Diamond, Muddy Waters and others, is now my most favorite DVD. Try this on for size, by the late singer/drummer Levon Helm, and if you understand these lyrics you deserve a medal:

> I pulled into Nazareth, was feelin' about half past dead;
> I just need some place where I can lay my head.
> "Hey, mister, can you tell me where a man might find a bed?"
> He just grinned and shook my hand, and "No!", was all he said.

> (Chorus:)

> Take a load off Fanny, take a load for free;
> Take a load off Fanny, And (and) (and) you can put the load right on me.

> I picked up my bag, I went lookin' for a place to hide;
> When I saw Carmen and the Devil walkin' side by side.
> I said, "Hey, Carmen, come on, let's go downtown."
> She said, "I gotta go, but m'friend can stick around."

> (Chorus)

> Go down, Miss Moses, there's nothin' you can say
> It's just ol' Luke, and Luke's waitin' on the Judgement Day.
> "Well, Luke, my friend, what about young Anna Lee?"
> He said, "Do me a favor, son, woncha stay an' keep Anna Lee company?"

> Crazy Chester followed me, and he caught me in the fog.
> He said, "I will fix your rack, if you'll take Jack, my dog."
> I said, "Wait a minute, Chester, you know I'm a peaceful man."
> He said, "That's okay, boy, won't you feed him when you can."

> (Chorus)

> Catch a cannon ball now, t'take me down the line

---

[8] I think Paul McCartney and John Lennon should be celebrated as the best songwriters since Hoagy Carmichael. That's not a fact, just an opinion, and Robbie Robertson of The Band is a close third, another opinion. The Band was collectively inducted into the Canadian Music Hall of Fame in 1989. See them on YouTube.

But in the Beatles' lyrics I still hear the story of my life, from "Norwegian Wood" to "This Is Not Dying." They truly have a song for my every mood, and I think Lennon's assassination was an incalculable tragedy for the music world.

My bag is sinkin' low and I do believe it's time.
To get back to Miss Fanny, you know she's the only one.
Who sent me here with her regards for everyone.[9]

Enigmatic lyrics. I mean, is Fanny the singer's girlfriend or his backside? Who is Anna Lee? And then crazy Chester at the end is a loose cannon. Perhaps it is a metaphor for the Christ story. After all, it starts out in Nazareth. Quite a mystery to me.

Okay, now this one is happier, with lyrics more accessible:

You can walk on the water, drown in the sand
You can fly off a mountaintop if anybody can
Run away, run away--it's the restless age
Look away, look away--you can turn the page
Hey, buddy, would you like to buy a watch real cheap
Here on the street
I got six on each arm and two more round my feet
Life is a carnival--believe it or not
Life is a carnival--two bits a shot

Saw a man with the jinx in the third degree
From trying to deal with people--people you can't see
Take away, take away, this house of mirrors
Give away, give away, all the souvenirs
We're all in the same boat ready to float off the edge of the world
The flat old world
The street is a sideshow from the peddler to the corner girl
Life is a carnival--it's in the book
Life is a carnival--take another look

Hey, buddy, would you like to buy a watch real cheap
Here on the street
I got six on each arm and two more round my feet
Life is a carnival--believe it or not
Life is a carnival--two bits a shot.[10]

****

---

[9] "The Weight," on *The Best of The Band,* lyrics by Levon Helm, Robbie Robertson, Rick Danko; Ascap.

[10] "Life Is a Carnival," ibid.

.

It is about twenty years now since I leaped out of bed at 6 a.m., eager for the day ahead. Nowadays I will get up if necessary, but I tend to work until three or four a.m. and then sleep till noon.

Anyway, today I woke up thinking of a friend of mine, a fetching, winsome young woman (handsome doesn't begin to describe her). I shall call her Belle, for she rings ever true.

Okay, now Belle was a single lass, mid-twenties, gainfully employed and more or less unattached. She went away for a weekend to the Caribbean, and the very first evening there she was swept off her feet by a soft-spoken compatriot who made such gentle and satisfying love with her that she became quite besotted.

Now, this is the best that can happen to a woman—or a man—at any age. I mean to remind you, I am all in favor of falling in love. I have been there a few times, and it always took me off the ground, made me feel happily sky-high, something like this:

> Fly me to the moon
> Let me play among the stars
> Let me see what spring is like
> On a, Jupiter and Mars
> In other words, hold my hand
> In other words, baby, kiss me
>
> Fill my heart with song
> And let me sing for ever more
> You are all I long for
> All I worship and adore
> In other words, please be true
> In other words, I love you
> In other words, I love you.[11]

The big problem, of course, is that passionate love seldom lasts. It often becomes indifference or leads to belligerence or acrimony between couples. This is not an opinion, it is a fact. Prisons are full of men—and some women too—who have beaten their partners to a pulp for wanting, or not, to make love. Not my fault, just the messenger.

---

[11] Frank Sinatra, "Fly Me To the Moon," lyrics by Cole Porter; Ascap.

****

I once woke up from a dream in which I was addressing the Psychological Club of Zurich, thus:

"I have been here for three hours and I am suffering from severe alcohol and nicotine withdrawal. It does not become you as Jungians to have a policy of zero tolerance toward drugs of choice."

I sat down amidst a strong round of applause and woke up to find myself staring at my iMac.

The dream is instructive. Besides exposing my literal stupidity, I think it compensates my feeling of alienation from the greater Jungian community, though I have no conscious desire to be part of it—other, of course, than what I put out into the world via Inner City Books. This is what occupies me in my turret: how to reconcile introversion with the extraverted wish to be part of a wider community. This issue is often addressed by other Jungians, so I will not belabor it here. But I would like to quote again my late mentor, Marie-Louise von Franz, as follows:

> Indeed, individuation is a solitary endeavor. It takes time away from family and friends. For this reason it is not popular in an extraverted culture. However, look deeper at individuation and you see that it actually brings one closer to the whole of humanity. Paradoxically, one can find in one's aloneness what is eternal and binds one to others. This is a precious discovery, not to be found in the hurly-burly of the marketplace. [12]

****

It is widely known that there is often a split in a man's psyche between woman as sex object and woman as mother. This means he may tend to put a woman on a pedestal on the one hand, and degrade her on the other; for instance, he can't make love to his adored partner, but he can make out with a "slut." This disparity may cause him a good deal of grief and conflict, and with any luck will take him into analysis, where he may discover the complexes behind his puzzling behavior patterns.

This is not to say that everyone is suited to analysis, or even needs it.

---

[12] *Individuation in Fairy Tales,* p. 45.

But for those in conflictual relationships, or indeed any conflict situation, Jungian analysis offers a way out of the morass. I would like to find something complimentary to say about Freudian analysis, but I know too many people who have been on the couch three or four times a week for twenty years, and are still as neurotically unhappy as ever.

I once had a middle-aged client, call him George, who for ten years obsessed over a woman, call her Clara, a feisty waif he met in a foreign country. They had a brief affair, after which he returned to Canada and they lost touch. Five years later George accidentally saw Clara on television, working in a different country. He tried to make contact, but was rebuffed several times. He wondered if he should fly to her and declare his love, although he was ambivalent about his feelings for her. For instance, if it turned out that she accepted him, he did not know what he would do with her....

It was a sticky wicket, for sure. George risked a further rejection if he went to her, and more repressed grief if he didn't. We discussed his options at length. I finally suggested that the problem was not whether he should go to her or not, but that he had no anchor, no center, in himself, according to which he might evaluate her worth to him. I encouraged him to write about the history of his obsession and become aware of the degree to which he had projected his own unconscious needs onto her. I also urged him to consult with his inner woman—ask her how she felt about the fantasy relationship he had developed with Clara, an essentially unknown woman.

This process took some months, but eventually George forged a relationship with his inner woman, a faceless wraith he called Clarissa. She advised him to sit tight and work on himself. The next step for George was to give a face to Clarissa. He drew and painted her visage over many weeks until she was burned into his heart. Eventually his longing for Clara dissipated, and George consigned her to the closet called experience. But his relationship with Clarissa continued and deepened, taking him into a realm of the mind he had never known existed—the unconscious pleroma that underpins and potentially invigorates us all.

I could cite more case material here, but I won't because readers may

20

be inclined to identify with them and thus be deflected from their personal task, which is to find out who they are—individuals different from anyone else. There are many obstacles in this endeavor, including cultural pressures and particularly the expectations of loved ones who may not understand or respect the solitary and adventurous process of individuation.

Just the messenger.

****

Well, that's enough Logos for now; let's hear some Eros from Madeleine Peyroux:

> Dance me to your beauty with a burning violin
> Dance me through the panic 'til I'm gathered safely in
> Lift me like an olive branch and be my homeward dove
> Dance me to the end of love, dance me to the end of love
>
> Oh let me see your beauty when the witnesses are gone
> Let me feel you moving like they do in Babylon
> Show me slowly what I only know the limits of
> Oh dance me to the end of love, dance me to the end of love
>
> Dance me to the wedding now, dance me on and on
> Dance me very tenderly and dance me very long
> We're both of us beneath our love, we're both of us above
> Dance me to the end of love, dance me to the end of love
>
> ....
>
> Dance me to your beauty with a burning violin
> Dance me through the panic till I'm gathered safely in
> Touch me with your naked hand or touch me with your glove
> Dance me to the end of love, dance me to the end of love
> Dance me to the end of love.[13]

And there you have it: there is no end to a dancing heart when you're in love.

---

[13] "Dance Me to the End of Love," lyrics by Leonard Cohen; Ascap.

2
HEDONISM

I am not, as I'd planned to be over Christmas, in Negril Village at the notorious half-nudist Hedonism II resort in Jamaica. I chose this all-inclusive vacation as compensation for my lonely, introverted turret. By all accounts, Hedonism II is a haven for puers and extraverts, and my Razr shadow wanted to live. Hear him speak now as if he went there.

****

On the beach I am surrounded by naked women. I would like to hook up with one, but they are mostly under thirty and unlikely to be interested in a balding old snort, nor me in them. I browse the beach for mature women close to my own age, and wonder how on earth to approach one.

"Hi there, Susan Sarandon looks a lot like you."

"Cameron Diaz has your legs."

"Hi there, love your outfit. What's your name? Can I buy you a free drink?"

"Pardon me, may I join you, or is this sand taken?"

After fruitless fantasies I lie down on a beach towel. I fall into a dreamy state until I feel a touch on my shoulder. I open my eyes to see a woman of a certain age plop down beside me. She touched my head.

"I saw you checking us out," she said. "I was sorry you passed me by."

"And why is that?" I asked.

"Most men here are jocks," she said, "little boys looking to get drunk and laid. I'm worth more than that, and you look like my kind of guy."

"Well said," I opined. "But I too like to make love."

"All in good time, my friend," she laughed. "Let's have a drink. I am Mary Lynn. Make mine rum and coke."

"Razr here, at your service," I said, choosing my usual *nom de guerre*. I trekked to the closest nude swim-up bar and picked up drinks. Mine was Johnny Walker Black choked with ice. It was noon and my first drink of the day.

Mary Lynn was lying on her back. Nothing on but Hugo Boss sunglasses. Toned body for a woman her age—more or less sixty, I guessed, but I can't tell anymore. Blonde hair turning white, but complexion right out of l'Oréal—a boomer, as they're called these days.

She sat up and sipped her drink. "I want you to know," she said, "that I am employed by this resort to make our guests feel welcome and comfortable, so they will come back again. But still, I am free to choose my companions. Today I have chosen you. And if it comes to making consensual love, that is part of the welcome wagon."[14] She paused. ""Personally, I long for an experienced, mature man to explore my mind and body, to appreciate me as I am, not his projected image of me."

I sat with Mary Lynn for about an hour. We applied sun lotion to each other and talked of books and psychology and sealing wax.

"Mary Lynn," I finally said, "you're my kind of girl. Come with me."

We picked up our towels and walked hand in hand to my room overlooking giant gardenias and eucalyptus. I mean, it felt like Paradise.

I helped Mary Lynn onto the bed and said, "Let's take our time. You are so beautiful, how do you stand it?"

She laughed. "I avoid mirrors."

I would like to have disrobed Mary Lynn, but she was already naked (the downside of being a nudist). I lay beside her and caressed her tanned body. She took hold of me and gentled me into shape.

"I fall in love too easily," I whispered, thinking of Chet Baker.

We frolicked until dawn, occasionally talking of Rilke, Carl Jung, Paul Tillich, Dave Brubeck, and the mysteries of love. She was clearly of my generation and no dummy.

"You are a gentle man, Mr. Razr," Mary Lynn said as she flitted out the door after a shower. "That was special fun. Sorry to leave, but I have an early shift today. See you on the beach."

Well, I slept until noon, emotionally and physically replete. Hedonism II, it's only Day Two of twelve and you have already surpassed my expectations. I check the "Daily Events" board to see what I might be missing. Snorkeling, fishing for tuna, sailing and scuba lessons. No thanks. But there is a toga party planned for the evening in the disco ballroom. I might be up for that after a nap. I was disco king in Zurich. Granted, that

---

[14] A wry reference to a routine American custom in the mid-twentieth century—greeting newcomers with a basket of goodies to welcome them to the neighborhood.

was forty-some years ago, but still, after a night with Mary Lynn, I'm as frisky as Seabiscuit. Feeling like Chet:

> I fall in love too easily
> I fall in love too fast
> I fall in love too terribly hard
> For love to ever last
>
> My heart should be well-schooled
> 'Cause I've been fooled in the past
> But still I fall in love so easily
> I fall in love too fast
>
> My heart should be well-schooled
> 'Cause I've been fooled in the past
> But still I fall in love too easily
> I fall in love too fast.[15]

****

Another day on the beach. More free Scotch, more naked ladies. Volleyball, badminton, billiards. D wanted a break from his lonely turret, and I'm getting it in spades. Come to think of it, we all looked like Chet Baker in the 1950s. Brylcream, a little dab'll do ya.

Now, extraversion is hard to fake. I wander about in my birthday suit and eye the pretty ladies in theirs. Thanks to Mary Lynn, I no longer feel like a fish out of water, but still, I don't have much energy in the sun after our night of loving. I go back to my room and pick up a book. I am lodged on the nude side of the resort, so couples passing by are a distraction, but I am fiercely interested in Jung's long essay on synchronicity. This concept has long been known to Orientals, but it has yet to sink into the Western consciousness, namely the idea that some happenings are "acausally connected," (i.e., not conjoined by cause and effect, as rational thinking has posited since the Renaissance).

Well, I could blather on here about synchronicity, but anything I'd write has already been said by Jung or pre-empted by J. Gary Sparks.[16]

****

---

[15] Chet Baker "I Fall In Love Too Easily," music and lyrics by Chet Baker; Ascap.

[16] See *At the Heart of Matter: Synchronicity and Jung's Spiritual Testament.*

24

The Band was a phenomenon that manifested in the 1960s and peaked at the legendary Woodstock festival in 1969. Their songs seem to come out of thin air, made up on the spot, but apparently they worked them over for months in an old farmhouse they called the Big Pink in Woodstock, New York, loaned to them by Bob Dylan. Such arcane details, and more, are divulged on the DVD by the lead singer and songwriter, Robbie Robertson, in conversation with Martin Scorsese, director of *The Last Waltz.* This film of the concert is an incomparable piece of work, creatively captured by Scorsese, and the DVD reveals much more of how it came to be. It is a must-see by fans of The Band.

After that monumental finale, members of The Band went their separate ways. Levon Helm, who recently died, 2011) sang solo and became an actor, notably as the father of Loretta Lynn, Sissy Spacek's academy-award-winning role in *The Coal Miner's Daughter;* Robbie has had an illustrious career song-writing and fronting various bands. Now, I don't know what happened to the others—Garth Hudson, eclectic fiddler/organist, and singer/guitarist Rick Danko. I could probably find out if I Googled them, but it's late and I don't have the energy to do that. Pardon me if I take a load off Fanny and go to bed. All the same, I am tempted to share one more Band song with you, according to my late-night Eros/puer mood:

> It makes no diff'rence where I turn
> I can't get over you and the flame still burns
> It makes no diff'rence, night or day
> The shadow never seems to fade away
>
> And the sun don't shine anymore
> And the rains fall down on my door
>
> Now there's no love
> As true as the love
> That dies untold
> But the clouds never hung so low before
>
> It makes no diff'rence how far I go
> Like a scar the hurt will always show
> It makes no diff'rence who I meet
> They're just a face in the crowd
> On a dead-end street
> And the sun don't shine anymore
> And the rains fall down on my door

These old love letters
Well, I just can't keep
'Cause like the gambler says
Read 'em and weep
And the dawn don't rescue me no more

Without your love I'm nothing at all
Like an empty hall it's a lonely fall
Since you've gone it's a losing battle
Stampeding cattle
They rattle the walls

And the sun don't shine anymore
And the rains fall down on my door

Well, I love you so much
It's all I can do
Just to keep myself from telling you
That I never felt so alone before

****

Well, that was a pleasant diversion, but now I must get back to what this book is purportedly about—growing up puer. So I think it's time to let my alter-ego/shadow Razr back into this discourse.

****

I was at loose ends some years ago when I came across, or rather stumbled upon, Emma Lou. My paramour of six years had gone back to her husband, and I didn't blame her for that. But I did feel bereft without someone to frolic with.

I am a man who needs a loving woman. This is not unusual for men, and not necessarily evidence of a puer syndrome. Everything depends on the context and the personal psychology.

Okay now, Emma Lou. It was twilight, loneliest time of day. I almost tripped over her as she was panhandling in Toronto on the corner of Queen Street west and John. She was playing a juice (Jew's) harp, not too badly. It's a very trendy area, and her cup was already half full with bills and coins. She was waifish, disheveled, hiding behind a cowboy hat. I liked her at once, thanks to my savior complex, which is, indeed, common to many puers—not my fault, I'm just the messenger. I am a real sucker for anyone who reminds me of Mimi in *La Bohème*.

I knelt down. "Hey there, little lady, what's your name?"

"Emma Lou," she shrugged, defensive. "Who wants to know?"

"I'm Razr," I said. "I have a mini-mansion in Rosedale. I could give you shelter."

"You won't hurt me, will you? she asked.

"No chance," I replied.

I helped Emma Lou to her feet. She gathered up her few things and the money basket and I popped her into my harvest gold VW.

I first took Emma Lou to my house, perhaps to show her that I was a man of means and meant no harm. I don't know if she knew, but Rosedale is a pretty pricey area of Toronto. Anyway, she seemed impressed by the oak staircase and artwork and kissed me heartily.

"Thank you," she breathed, "you are a good man."

Well, we'd see about that later, for I was already thinking of tearing her clothes off. But after touring my house, I steered Emma Lou to my favorite local Thai restaurant. We feasted and walked back to my house hand in hand. I always like that feeling of intimacy.

At home, I filled up my tiny new 4-cup Betty Crocker machine. We were quiet, sipping decaf and Cointreau. I did not press her for the circumstances that found her on the street. Well, I may have a savior complex, but I'm not the Grand Inquisitor or the angel Gabriel.

"It's bin a long day," said Emma Lou finally, "I'm so tired."

"Yes, my dear," I said. "Come, I will care for you."

I led Emma Lou to the master bedroom, where I tucked her in under the duvet and kissed her chastely. "Sweet dreams," I said, "I shall be upstairs."

"Oh Mister Razr, don't leave me," she begged. "I bin so scared and lonely."

Well, I am a gentleman, first and last. I undressed, pulled back the elephant-coded covers, and settled in beside Emma Lou.

"You smell so good, like jasmine and cocoa butter," I whispered, "and you saved me from jumping offa bridge."

"Me too, you silly," she said, and then. "Are you into foreplay?" she asked shyly.

"You bet," I replied, "until the cows come home."

And so we did until falling asleep at dawn.

This seemed to suit us both, and before I knew it the alarm was buzzing, for I had a client at 9 a.m.

We made love thereafter occasionally, but not seriously. In her thirties, Emma Lou married an acrobat in the Cirque du Soleil and bore him adorable twin girls, Gabriella and Sophia.

****

That was all puer fantasy, of course. Razr's encounter with Emma Lou didn't happen apart from his lascivious imagination. Now, that isn't to say she wasn't real, only that she is a metaphor for men's instinctive appetite.

I should explain, since some readers may not have learned to parse a sentence, which means to identify its constituent parts. I will simplify the sentence for illustration, thus:

"Emma Lou is a metaphor for men's instinctive appetite."

Here, "Emma Lou" is a compound proper noun and subject of the sentence. "Is" is a verb, transitive (meaning it takes an object). The word "a" is an indefinite article (compared to "the," a definite article). Now here comes the object, "metaphor," a noun, followed by a prepositional phrase—"for" being the preposition, and "men's instinctive appetite" being the phrasal-object of the preposition.

Now, if that is clear, we can move on to bigger and better things. For instance, what is a metaphor? And why is Emma Lou described as such?

Okay, simply said, according to the *American Heritage dictionary* a metaphor is "a symbol or representation for something else," and Jung defines a symbol as the best formulation for something essentially unknown.[17] So Emma Lou in the context is, figuratively (i.e., not literally) a sex object, but metaphorically, symbolically, she could be any woman. She could be called Daisy Mae or Lorraine or Bo Peep, makes no difference. "Instinctive" means innate/inborn, and "appetite" is also a figure of speech referring to what men like. Razr did not literally eat Emma Lou. He only desired to couple with her.

I don't mean to be provocative, but did Emma Lou and Razr do something wrong? They saved each other from suicidal jumps offa bridge and had a pleasant coital cuddle. This has been going on for millennia. Feminists may not like it, but women are naturally sex objects for men, and

---

[17] "Definitions," *Psychological Types,* CW 6, pars. 814ff.

attempts to "desexualize" their breasts or buttocks won't change that. I am of course supportive of feminism, but with a few caveats.

Perhaps the main problem for the puer is that he often can't tell the difference between "figurative" and "literal." And, indeed, who can?

Case rests, yer Honor.

****

There once was an older woman
who passed by
from time to time. (By older
I mean more or less my own age,
no spring chicken).
Anyway, one day she saw me struggling
up the porch steps with a bag of groceries
in one hand, a cane in the other,
and she rushed over to help me.
That's how we met.

I was grateful and invited her in
for coffee and a chat.
I had no intention
of molesting her, nor did I that.
We relaxed in the leather chairs
in which I sit opposite a client
delving into the unconscious. But
I did not ask if she dreamed.

"My name is Natalie," she said shyly.
I was immediately taken back in time.
I said, "Do you remember Bob & Ray,
A comedy team in the 1960s?"
"No," she giggled.
"Well," I observed, "they had
an imaginary girl friend they called
Natalie Attired. Always broke me up."

Natalie did not stay long enough
For Razr to give her a hug,
and just as well. We remain

passing friends to this very day,
and Eros reigns supreme.

Now, you may well ask, why didn't Razr make a move on the elderly Ms. Natalie Attired? Well, perhaps she didn't stir his male libido, or he sensed it would be unwelcome, and/or he was not inclined to be known as the neighborhood letch. Perhaps he was even growing up puer.

Razr is uncharacteristically mute on the subject, so it's all a mystery to me.

****

Last night I did finally watch the movie *My Week with Marilyn* (2011), purporting to document a young man's experience with Marilyn as she struggled to make a film in England in 1956.

Well, what a romp! Michelle Williams as Marilyn is adorable and she does a terrific job of emulating the real Monroe's sexy and sensuous but fragile persona. Kenneth Branagh is also excellent as Lawrence Olivier, her director and costar in the putative film they're supposed to be making together. It may be *The Sleeping Prince,* or finally *The Prince and the Showgirl,* I lost track.

No matter, Marilyn and Sir Lawrence did not get along. She was a rising star in the Hollywood culture, and he was an icon of the London stage. She wished to show that she could act; he wanted to transfer his stage skills to film. They repeatedly and foreseeably clashed. She was always late for rehearsals and scheduled scenes, forgot her lines, and he was left fuming. Olivier's wife at the time, Vivian Leigh, is shown as fearful that he would fall in love with Marilyn, which he shrugs off with the wry comment to the diarist Colin Clark, "Remember boy [puer], when it comes to women, you're never too old for humiliation."

Meanwhile, in the back story that is the basis and heart of this film, the young Colin (twenty-three), fortuitously taken on as the film's Third Assistant Director (meaning gopher/go for coffee or whatever else we tell you to do), becomes the thirty-one year old Marilyn's best friend and in thrall to her, especially when she entices him to swim nude in a lake. In the end, Marilyn returns to New York and her husband at that time

30

(the acclaimed playwright Arthur Miller), and Colin tries to reestablish his budding romance with the cute stage-hand Nikki whom he likes but has neglected because of his feelings for Marilyn.

Well, it is finally a touching and sad film in that it cuts so close to the bone in terms of our projections onto movie stars and how that affects them. For instance, we are shown Marilyn vamping for crowds and loving the attention, but unable to sleep alone without a cocktail of pills. So she often calls on Colin to keep her company (apparently simply as an affectionate presence with whom she feels safe). "I'll fall in love with you," she says, "because I always do." Of course, Colin melts, for by then he has seen her naked more than once and is totally smitten.

Personally, I grew up with Marilyn Monroe as familiar as a postage stamp, and I enjoyed *My Week with Marilyn* immensely. Her last words to Colin are, "Please don't forget me." He replies, "As if I could." And I feel the same, as do millions of others.

In 1957, the following year, back in America, Monroe made *Some Like It Hot* with Tony Curtis and Jack Lemon, perhaps her best film, while Olivier outdid himself in the award-winning *The Entertainer*.

Marilyn Monroe has since the 1950s personified an archetypal image of the feminine—desirable but unattainable, wounded and wounding.

Now, it took more than sixty years before the then young star-struck Colin decided to allow his experience with Marilyn to be documented and reenacted. I don't know why it took so long, but and I'm very glad he finally did; also that the great, prolific film producer Harvey Weinstein recognized the story's worth and put it out to the world.

Just saying, with love to all.

3
PUER REDUX

Now, as for the subtitle of this book, according to what I have already written, juxtaposing "Growing Up" and "Puer" may seem oxymoronic. But consider the mistaken belief that adolescence must be outgrown before one grows up. Au contraire; psychologically, the essence of the puer must accompany a man as he ages or he becomes dry, listless, and spiritless—the essence of negative senex (old man), not wise, but rather crotchety and irritable.

Bob Dylan expresses this as well as anyone with these lyrics:

> May God bless and keep you always
> May your wishes all come true
> May you always do for others
> And let others do for you
> May you build a ladder to the stars
> And climb on every rung
> May you stay forever young
> May you stay forever young.
>
> May you grow up to be righteous
> May you grow up to be true
> May you always know the truth
> And see the lights surrounding you
> May you always be courageous
> Stand upright and be strong
> May you stay forever young
> May you stay forever young.
>
> May your hands always be busy
> May your feet always be swift
> May you have a strong foundation
> When the winds of changes shift
> May your heart always be joyful
> And may your song always be sung
> May you stay forever young.
> May you stay forever young. [18]

---

[18] "Forever Young," lyrics by Dylan; Ascap.

That is like Gepetto advising Pinocchio (in some versions of the tale) to "Stay wood!"[19] And what is the "essence of the puer"? Well, he may be fickle and unable to commit himself to just one woman, but on the positive side there is his love of life, his spontaneity, his creative drive and an urge to excel himself—or better said, the need to realize his potential. This is not easily done, and seldom without a professional companion on the perilous journey of getting to know oneself.

This journey is perilous because it involves acknowledging one's shadowy side and becoming familiar with the inner woman or man in oneself. No getting around it—this can be a scary experience, not for the faint of heart.

****

The thing is, I've suddenly forgotten what I had in mind to add here. So, welcome to the pleroma, the vast unconscious, where anything goes and anything can happen outside of time and space (as in dreams). As a young person, you can put it all out there and see who bites; as an older gent, like me, you tend to sleep till noon and not care one way or another.

****

I receive hundred of emails every day from all over the world and from all kinds of people and businesses. Some are orders for books, so I have to sift through them all, in spite of Mac's mail program's filters. And there are often gems to put in my next book.

Today my favorite is one touting the "Genie Bra," featuring "woven everlast technology, wide comfort lift band, no wires or hooks, and soft, full coverage lift cups." There is an attractive buxom lady modestly modeling the bra, and by the way it's an exclusive offer: "buy 3, get 3 free." Just what I need to set me up for the day's routine work.

I needn't mention all the dating sites enticing me to service lonely married women, for everyone gets those. I have an instinctively libidinous response to the wares on display by the handsome sexy ladies, and I have fantasies, but I don't act on them. I spend hours each day deleting such messages, for my heart currently belongs to the numinous Bo Peep. Which means I won't soon be planking any local lonely married women.

---

[19] See my *Dear Gladys: The Survival Papers, Book 2,* pp. 133ff.

33

That is love, loyalty, romance and Eros. Without my distant Bo Peep, I could cut a charming swath through those lonely ladies, at the cost of my soul. All said, that is Razr's domain, not mine. This too is growing up puer—putting relationship before desire.

Okay Razr, give it your best shot.

****

I went to my local pharmacy last week to pick up some personal items, toothpaste, mouthwash, etc. Then I spotted the pharmacist, a cute middle-aged woman with a killer smile. I ambled up to her counter and noted her name-tag.

I flashed my fake store-security badge.

"Amy," I said, "I have an ED problem."

"Mister Razr, there are medications for erectile dysfunction," said Amy, "but you'd need a doctor's prescription."

I leaned toward her. "Amy, I have the pills, Viagra, Cialis, and some nameless naturopathic substance from Ecuador. My problem is that I lack a woman to use them with."

Amy touched my hand. "Hang on, Mister Razr, I soon have a break for fifteen minutes."

I hung around until Amy emerged from the pharmacy with a bright smile. She took my hand and guided me to a quiet corner in the store's catacombs.

"Let's call this synchronicity," she said, shedding her white outfit, "I too have needed some loving."

We coupled with as much ardor as we could in the confined space. I was reluctant to let her go, but Amy was adamant.

"Mister Razr, that was fun but it was a one-time thing. Let's not pretend otherwise. Merry Christmas."

She left and I pulled myself together. I don't understand women, but I do love them yet.

****

I was speaking with my close friend and colleague Rebecca the other day about my *Eros Trilogy*.

"You invented Razr to give voice to your own libidinous preoccupations," she said. "Is that correct?"

34

I hugged Rebecca. "Yes, that is more or less true."

She clung to me. "Are you not more conscious than that?"

I rocked Rebecca on her low heels as we slow-danced in the kitchen to Duke Ellington. I was not anxious to tussle with her animus, but Rachel came forward to help me.

"My dear," I said, "don't confuse your personal beliefs with the absolute truth. You seem to feel that being conscious means not thinking about sex—while I believe that thinking about sex has nothing to do with consciousness, but is rather a consequence of not getting enough of it. And besides, Razr deserves some respect. He is, after all, ten million years old."

"You may be right," Rebecca reluctantly conceded, flashing her green eyes and smiling. "I might take you to bed if I wasn't getting enough."

"I will look forward to that," I took her hand and bowed. Fat chance, I thought, for she was married to a robust freedom fighter and golf champ from Liberia. A Schwarzenegger lookalike, he could snap me in two with the flick of a thick wrist.

Take a load off Fanny, indeed.

****

4
TURRET HEAD

"A young man serves his country,
And an old man guards his home."[20]

I was asleep and woken by a knock at the door at 3 a.m. Having that very day read of home invasions, I dared not open the door. I called the police and they said they'd send a cruiser to the neighborhood. Five minutes later I received a phone call from a taxi driver waiting in my driveway with his lights off. He said he had been dispatched to my address. I chewed him out a bit before realizing it was some kind of mix-up, for I *had* ordered a cab, but *yesterday* for 3 *p.m.* I called the police again and cancelled the distress call. Then I called the taxi company and gave the dispatcher merry hell. He apologized profusely for his computer glitch. I told him to get a new effing computer or another job.

Now I ask you, Rebecca, what does it all mean? I only stay sane by Scotching, Drumming, and listening to the Beatles or The Band:

> It makes no difference where I turn,
> I can't get over you, and the flame still burns.
> It makes no difference night or day,
> The shadows never seem to fade away.
> And the sun don't shine any more,
> And the rains fall down on my door......
> It's all I can do to keep from loving you......
> And I never felt so alone before......
> Cause the sun don't rescue me no more,
> And the rains fall down on my door.....[21]

Not my fault, only the messenger.

Happy Easter and I love you.

---

[20] "Twilight," on *The Best of The Band;* Ascap.
[21] "It Makes No Difference," ibid.

5
DATING SITES

Razr barged in, steaming. He banged his head against the wall. Twice. Bong! Bong!

"Hey Bud," I said, "what's up with you?"

"I bin checkin' out dating sites," He shook his head.

"Wha?"

"Well, I shoulda knowed better," said Razr. "What self-respecting woman puts herself out to the world as "HornyLorna," "Sexyforyou babe" or "Hotandhorny girl"?

I slapped him. "So what did you do?"

Razr ground his teeth and looked at me. "I fell for it. I finally chose a site that looked pretty sexy and I took out a free 3-day trial membership. I quickly learned that you can see many captivating lovelies in your area for free, but you can't communicate with them unless you actually pay for a subscription. So I joined for a week, browsed the provocative profiles, and emailed a few lovelies to hook up for coffee, have a drink, take a walk, get to know each other, like that. I sent kisses, flirts, chocolates, flowers, and etc. Three days later, no responses, not even a courtesy note, from any of them. Then it struck me: these lovelies were shills for the site, bait to keep men renewing their memberships. So I cancelled my subscription, with a sharp note to the so-called Support Team."

I shrugged. "Well, what have you lost?"

"$21.50, and my self-respect!" cried Razr, wringing his hands. "But I got my revenge."

"How?"

Razr rubbed his hands. "I went on the Internet to scam.com and recounted my experience. And there, as it happens, I found other gents, and women too, reporting similar experience and suspicions."

"Jeez," I said, "what will they think of next?"

6
JIMMY KRACK KORN

Yesterday afternoon I leaned too far back in my office chair and it scooted out from under me. I hit my left side on the hard corner of an open drawer, then fell to the floor. My side began to hurt something awful and I had a restless sleep disturbed by gargoyles. Worse this morning; it hurts to breathe, to cough, to bend, to reach out, to straighten up, sit down, get up. On the usual scale of 1-10, I give it about 11½. Not such a hurt since my ankle was fractured and I was abducted up to Aliensville (the Mother Ship). So today I went to my chiropractor, who gave me a requisition for an x-ray, which I duly had and confirmed the feeling that I have a cracked rib. My doc tells me it will heal in a week or two or three; no treatment required except Tylenol and daily applications of magnesium oil and/or the naturopathic calendula cream.

Of course, I am professionally trained to be skeptical about so-called accidents and I must entertain the possibility of synchronicity, where what is happening inside is mirrored by an outside event (i.e., the mysterious connection between psyche and matter).[22] Now, even though in this instance there was obviously cause and effect at work—my leaning back caused the upset—I am obliged to consider it also as a synchronous event, what Jung calls an "acausal coincidence," just to cover all the bases, for in fact I have been "bending over backwards," so to speak, to create a comfortable, commodious ensuiteheart for a visit from the ephemeral Ms. Bo Peep. It also means I have to consider my personal associations to chair, drawer and rib, plus their symbolic and mythological amplifications; e.g., the Biblical tale of Adam's rib being used to create woman.

This process is what is known as "working on oneself." In so doing we may discover that the unconscious tripped us up. Or as the French

---

[22] See J. Gary Sparks, *At the Heart of Matter: Synchronicity and Jung's Spiritual Testament.*

writer René Daumal figuratively put it:

> Never halt on a shifting slope. Even if you think you have a firm foothold, as you take time to catch your breath and have a look at the sky, the ground will settle little by little under your weight; the gravel will begin to slip imperceptibly, and suddenly it will drop away under you and launch you like a ship. The mountain is always watching for a chance to give you a spill.[23]

The unconscious (or mountain; what's in a name?) is an awesome reality. Jung likened its vastness to that of the sea, for the contents of both are inexhaustible. Freud saw the unconscious, or subconscious, as little more than a garbage can of fantasies and emotions that were active when we were children and then were repressed or forgotten. Jung championed Freud's dogma for a while, but finally couldn't accept it because it didn't accord with his own experience. Jung came to believe instead that the unconscious also includes contents we never knew were there: things about ourselves in our personal unconscious, and then, at a deeper level, the collective unconscious—all the varied experiences of the human race, the stuff of myth, legend and religion—a vast historical warehouse. Under the right circumstances, any of this, at any time, can become conscious. Jung writes:

> Everything of which I know, but of which I am not at the moment thinking; everything of which I was once conscious but have now forgotten; everything perceived by my senses, but not noted by my conscious mind; everything which, involuntarily and without paying attention to it, I feel, think, remember, want, and do; all the future things that are taking shape in me and will sometime come to consciousness: all this is the content of the unconscious.[24]

And that is why, in spite of our best efforts, we will all, always, be more or less unconscious and prone to fall off chairs. We survive this human plight by escaping into sexual activity and entertainment media—

---

[23] *Mount Analogue: An Authentic Narrative,* p. 105.
[24] "On the Nature of the Psyche," *The Structure and Dynamics of the Psyche,* CW 8, par. 382.

movies, television, spectacles, circuses, sports, video games, etc.—and perhaps above all by singing to loved ones, like this:

If you go away
On this summer's day
Then you might as well
Take the sun away
All the birds that flew
In the summer sky
When our love was new
And our hearts were high
And the day was young
And the nights were long
And the moon stood still
For the night bird's song

If you go away
If you go away
If you go away...

But if you stay
I'll make you a day
Like no day has been
Or will be again
We'll sail on the sun
We'll ride on the rain
And talk to the trees
And worship the wind

But if you go
I'll understand
Leave me just enough love
To fill up my hand
If you go away
If you go away
If you go away...

If you go away
As I know you will
You must tell the world

To stop turning
'til you return again
If you ever do
For what good is love
Without loving you?
Can I tell you now
As you turn to go
I'll be dying slowly
'til the next hello

If you go away
If you go away
If you go away...

But if you stay
I'll make you a night
Like no night has been
Or will be again
I'll sail on your smile
I'll ride on your touch
I'll talk to your eyes
That I love so much

But if you go
I won't cry
Though the good is gone
From the word goodbye

If you go away
If you go away
If you go away...

If you go away
As I know you must
There is nothing left
In this world to trust
Just an empty room
Full of empty space
Like the empty look
I see on your face
And I'd been the shadow

Of your shadow
If you might have kept me
By your side

If you go away
If you go away
If you go away...

If you go away
If you go away...[25]

Surely one of the saddest songs ever writ. But consider this: when one goes out, another comes knocking at the door—life and love renewed.

And so the world turns, with us on it; we can only hope we don't fall off.

---

[25] Barbra Streisand, "If You Go Away *(Ne Me Quitte Pas)*"; Ascap.

7
EROS = SOPHIA BECOMING

Feeling derelict and dissolute, I spent a pleasant evening with my friend Rebecca, talking of our lives and sealing wax. Rebecca is happily married, and, as I've said, ours is a chaste friendship. Now, my inner woman Rachel is sometimes jealous—for she indulges herself by imagining that *she* (Rachel) is Sophia, famed consort of God and King Solomon—but she soon gets over it.

Now, Rebecca is as beautiful as any movie star who ever walked the red carpet on Oscar night. We desire without physical intimacy. I romance her to pieces by holding hands and massaging her feet. We are happy sharing a bottle of wine, listening to Dave Brubeck or Dinah Washington, or just staring at the wall. We smile and laugh a lot.

Rebecca is my confidante; I can tell her anything. We supervise each others' clients, and she gives me sound counsel regarding my presumptive paramours. I am in awe of Rebecca/Sophia. She is highly intuitive and so apprehends things that entirely escape my notice; thus I take her thoughts and advice very seriously. (She is after all known as Wisdom in the Bible.)[26] It is erotic and sensuous just being together without a bedroom agenda. Call it a trystNot. I am romantically passionate about my friend Rebecca but not lustful. It is a higher clime of love making.

Rebecca personifies for me the essence of the feminine: her looks, her clothes, her smell, her touch, her walk, her talk. Now, she is a woman onto whom I project Sophia, and so she (Rebecca) becomes that, and so my anima cloaks herself in that wonder, which manifests in me as an attentive interlocutor with no thoughts of undressing her. And the funny thing is, after a few hours with my under-cover loverNot, I feel as if we *are* lovers. I wish every man might experience this—carnal love subsumed by a soulful connection. Of course, it takes some restraint and psychological awareness on both sides. But that's what Sophia is all about.

---

[26] See esp. Proverbs 8:22-31.

I don't know about Rebecca, but Sophia does not shrink from consummating relationships when appropriate. Indeed, it is between the sheets that Sophia really shines; shy but forthcoming, she gives and receives with equal ardor. Further, she is monogamous but not possessive, receptive without being devouring; always helpful, thoughtful and affectionate. She expresses criticism warmly. She is fun to be with, and, with apologies to dogs, she is in fact a man's best friend.

My relationship with Rebecca/Sophia is Eros requited and undiluted by acrimony or sentimentality. It feels something like this:

> Deep within your heart, you know it's plain to see
> Like Adam was to Eve, you were made for me
> They say the poisoned vine breeds a finer wine
> Our love is easy
>
> If you ask me plainly I would gladly say
> I'd like to have you round just for them rainy days
> I like the touch of your hand, the way you make no demands
> Our love is easy
>
> Our love is easy
> Like water rushing over stone
> Oh, our love is easy, like no love I've ever known
>
> Physically speaking we were made to last
> Examine all the pieces of our recent past
> There's your mouth of tears
> Your hands around my waist
> Our love is easy
>
> -------------------------------------
>
> Deep within your heart, you know it's plain to see
> Like Adam was to Eve, you were made for me
> They say the poisoned vine breeds a finer wine
> Our love is easy.[27]

****

---

[27] Melody Gardot, "Our Love Is Easy," on *My One and Only Thrill*; music and lyrics by Gardot and Jesse Harris; © Old Edward Music Publishing; WB Music Corp.

I once had a friend named David Peel. He was offended when I took to calling him Orange. From him I learned that peoples' names are not something to toy with; they are akin to a sacred badge of identity.

What's in a name? Shakespeare's Juliet famously says to Romeo: "That which we call a rose / By any other name would smell as sweet."[28]

And don't forget the line sometimes attributed to Gertrude Stein's life-long companion Alice B. Toklas, immortalized in Stein's poem "Sacred Emily":

> Rose is a rose is a rose is a rose
> Loveliness extreme.
> Extra gaiters,
> Loveliness extreme.
> Sweetest ice-cream.
> Pages ages page ages page ages.[29]

So what's in a name? My point here is that Rebecca = Sophia = Eros.

****

Now, I have written at length about my relationship with Rebecca (code-named Nurse Pam in *The SleepNot Trilogy*),[30] but I have a bit more to say here about Sophia. She is the gentlest and most forgiving of creatures. She includes in herself all the earlier stages of a man's anima development (Eve, mother; Helen, sexuality; Mary, spiritual). She is indeed wise beyond her years and said to have been co-existent with God at the Creation, a possibly apocryphal fact that has enticed feminists to call God She. Well, I won't go there, but simply note that *Sophia* is the Greek word for wisdom, and the modern goddess cult owes much to the Gnostic belief that Sophia was a fourth member left out of the Trinity by the early patriarchal Church Fathers. This was formally, if belatedly, recognized by the Catholic Church in a 1950 Papal Bull by Pope Pius XII proclaiming the Assumption of the Blessed Virgin Mary into Heaven. Jung

---

[28] *Romeo and Juliet* (II, ii, 1-2).

[29] Written in 1913 and published in 1922, in *Geography and Plays*.

[30] Comprised of *Not the Big Sleep, On Staying Awake,* and *Eyes Wide Open.*

applauded this momentous event as symbolically signifying "the recognition and acknowledgement of matter."[31] In his autobiography, Jung is more explicit:

> The new dogma affirms that Mary as the Bride is united with the son in the heavenly bridal chamber, and as Sophia (Wisdom) she is united with the Godhead. Thus the feminine principle is brought into immediate proximity with the masculine Trinity.[32]

And thus more grounds for seeing God as She, for those who have had quite enough of the nasty or indifferent side of Yahweh, who did not stop the Holocaust or multiple wars all over the world, and gave Job such a hard time.[33]

Now, men, you don't need my Rebecca to celebrate Sophia. Turn to your own beloved and listen to her travails instead of taking your pleasure in haste. Find out who she is besides lover, mother, housekeeper. What is in her head, her heart? She will reward you ten-fold with wisdom you cannot otherwise acquire. See Sophia in your partner and she will become that numinous personification of the feminine.

****

Time for a song from the mighty Beatles' archive:

> Close your eyes and I'll kiss you,
> Tomorrow I'll miss you;
> Remember I'll always be true.
> And then while I'm away,
> I'll write home ev'ry day,
> And I'll send all my loving to you.
>
> I'll pretend I am kissing
> the lips I am missing
> And hope that my dreams will come true.

---

[31] "Psychological Aspects of the Mother Archetype," *The Archetypes and the Collective Unconscious,* CW 9i, par. 197.

[32] *Memories, Dreams, Reflections,* p. 202n.

[33] See Jung, "Answer to Job," *Psychology and Religion,* CW 11, and Edward F. Edinger, *Transformation of the God-Image: An Elucidation of Jung's* Answer to Job. (CW refers throughout to *The Collected Works of C.G. Jung)*

And then while I'm away,
I'll write home ev'ry day,
And I'll send all my loving to you.

All my loving I will send to you.
All my loving, darling I'll be true.

Close your eyes and I'll kiss you,
Tomorrow I'll miss you:
Remember I'll always be true.
And then while I'm away,
I'll write home ev'ry day,
And I'll send all my loving to you

All my loving I will send to you.
All my loving darling I'll be True.
All my loving All my loving ooh
All my loving I will send to you.[34]

I can hardly get enough of those four mop-heads, who take my heart where brains would not go. Well, we are all a bundle of contradictions. There is no position without its negation. For every yea in the psyche there is a nay, like the Chinese concept of yin/yang—in yin (feminine) there is a bit of yang (masculine), and in yang a bit of yin. In human beings, Eros and Logos is a balance constantly orchestrated by the Self, unseen and usually unacknowledged regulating center of the psyche, commonly experienced when it tugs us off our ego-desired track, or dumps us off a chair. Some people call it "a higher power" or "God," but what's in a name?

****

"How do you write?" I am sometimes asked. Well, often in my head, at night, after I've gone to bed. I either write something down, or try to remember it for the morning. It is a mug's game, but for me, for the past fifty years, the only game in town.

---

[34] "All My Loving," on *With the Beatles* (1963), lyrics by John Lennon, Paul Winston, Paul McCartney, Paul James; Ascap. It is said that this song was playing on the sound system at Roosevelt Hospital emergency when Lennon was pronounced dead after being shot in December, 1980 (Wikipedia).

8
GROWING UP PUER

My addiction to the writing process all started with my fascination for a group of philosopher-writers collectively, or academically, known as "the modern European mind"—Albert Camus, Samuel Beckett, Franz Kafka, Soren Kierkegaard, D.H. Lawrence, Henry Miller, John Paul Sartre, Simone de Beauvoir, Rainer Maria Rilke, and many others. Rilke's peripatetic love-life astonished me and I followed his path off and on. Sartre's weighty thoughts bewildered me but I naively took up the cudgel as an existentialist. Kafka's depressive *Diaries* took me by storm and I emulated his angst until after some years of Jungian analysis I had a psychological understanding of him that eventually became my Zurich thesis and my first published book, *The Secret Raven: Conflict and Transformation in the Life of Franz Kafka.* Then in 1980 I stumbled upon my métier, which was to publish books written by myself and other analysts promoting the ideas of Carl Jung. This arcane niche business has been successful enough to keep me in vegetables and from jumping offa bridge. But along the way, I did jump ship from Logos to Eros, from existentialism to essentialism,[35] and here I find myself today, with miles to go before I sleep. Give me a good sentence and I can write three pages. Of course it is often not worth a damn, but then I start again. I am not famous, but I am prolific.

That is the brief story of my "growing up puer."

****

Yes, it may seem oxymoronic to juxtapose "growing up" with "puer," but I can assure you it is not. The two go together like salt and pepper,

---

[35] Logos is of the mind; Eros is of the heart. And I am grateful to my colleague J. Gary Sparks for his succinct distinction between existentialism and essentialism: "The former holds that we create ourselves; the latter says that we rediscover ourselves (our original essence)." *(At the Heart of Matter: Synchronicity and Jung's Spiritual Testament,* pp. 127ff)

fish and chips, knife and fork, tea and sympathy, and stormy weather. Growing up often means simply getting older, but along the way, if we keep our wits about us and continue searching for our truth, nuggets of wisdom may accrete like barnacles.

What is the essence of growing up? Well, it is a life-long task for many men (and women too), for it involves leaving dependence on the parental home, assuming personal responsibility for one's life, missteps and all. And yet it is always contaminated by the puer/puella syndrome, the desire to fly free as a bird, irresponsible, magically protected by the gods from hurtful strife in daily life.

You see, my turret is pretty safe, but permeable to deep-seated insecurity and the general angst that accumulates over the years in a solitary, introverted individual.

Just saying.

****

I have resigned myself to living another ten years, Dea concedente. This has a lot of consequences, which I haven't figured out yet. I'll let you know when I do.

I was with my cute young dental hygienist today. I expected her to chide me because she could tell I haven't been flossing. Well, that's the flip side of a positive mother complex (that is, anticipating a woman's wrath). However, she didn't comment, only offered me a new toothbrush. But we both know one thing is sure: if I don't soon learn to floss, after seventy years of unsuccessfully trying, I will lose my remaining teeth.

9
SHADOWY BUSINESS

To the degree that we identify with a bright and blameless persona, our shadow is correspondingly dark. The persona may aim at perfection. The shadow reminds us we are simply human.

Everything about ourselves that we are not conscious of is shadow. Psychologically, the shadow opposes and compensates the persona, the "I" we show to the outside world. Where we are concerned to put on a good front, to do what is considered by others to be right and proper, our shadow is not. The realization of how and when our shadow enters our life, and at times takes over, is a precondition for self-knowledge and individuation. The more we become conscious of our shadow's intentions and behavior, the less of a threat it is and the more psychologically substantial we become. Jung writes:

> The shadow is a moral problem that challenges the whole ego-personality . . . . To become conscious of it involves recognizing the dark aspects of the personality as present and real.[36]

In Jung's description, the shadow, or at least its dark side, is composed of morally inferior wishes and motives, childish fantasies and resentments, etc.—all those things about ourselves we are not proud of and regularly seek to hide from others. For instance, in civilized societies aggression is a prominent aspect of the shadow, simply because it is not socially acceptable; it is nipped in the bud in childhood and its expression in adult life is met with heavy sanctions. The same is true of sexual behavior that deviates from the collective norm.

By and large, then, the shadow is a hodge-podge of repressed desires and "uncivilized" impulses. It is possible to become conscious of these, but in the meantime they are projected onto others. Just as we may mistake a real man or woman for the soul mate we yearn for, so we see our

---

[36] "The Shadow," *Aion,* CW 9ii, par. 14.

devils, our shadow, in others. This is responsible for much acrimony in personal relationships. On a collective level it gives rise to political polarization, wars and the ubiquitous practice of scapegoating.[37]

Realizing our shadow is not easy because we tend to cling to our persona, the ideal image we have of ourselves, which in a culture based on Judeo-Christian values is heavily influenced by the thou-shalt-nots enshrined in the Ten Commandments.

In everyday life, we do many things under the influence of a shadow fed up with the persona. We cheat on our tax returns; we lie, steal, kill and sleep with our neighbor's wife. When called to account, we are shamefaced and wonder who did it.

There is no generally effective way to assimilate the shadow. It is more like diplomacy or statesmanship, and it is always an individual matter. Shadow and ego are like two political parties jockeying for power. If one can speak of a technique at all, it consists solely in an attitude.

First, one has to accept and take seriously the existence of the shadow. You do this by taking note of how others react to you and you to them. Second, one has to become aware of the shadow's qualities and intentions. You discover this through conscientious attention to moods, fantasies and impulses. (Best to write them down, for future reference.) Third, a lengthy process of negotiation between you-as-you'd-like-to-be and you-as-you'd-rather-not-be is unavoidable.

On the other hand, the shadow is not only the dark underside of the conscious personality. It also has a bright side: aspects of ourselves that comprise our unlived life—talents and abilities that have long been buried or never been conscious; part and parcel of who we are meant to be. They are potentially available, and their conscious realization often releases a surprising amount of energy. That is why, in Jungian analysis, a depressed or fearful person is counseled to go into their fear or depression rather than try to escape it. "Going into" a mood means confronting it. Don't identify with it; give it a name and dialogue with it. The buried treasure in our moods can only be unearthed by conscious effort.

---

[37] See Sylvia Brinton Perera, *The Scapegoat Complex: Toward a Mythology of Shadow and Guilt.*

51

Personally, in dialoguing with any particular shadow inclination of my own, I find it helpful, in deciding whether or not to act it out, to have at least these questions in mind:

1) Is it legal?
2) Could it endanger my life?
3) How might it affect my loved ones?
4) Could I live with the consequences?

A psychological crisis activates both sides of the shadow: those qualities and activities we are not proud of, and possibilities we never knew or have forgotten were there. Associated with the former—according to consciously-held moral values—is a sense of shame and distaste. The latter may have morally neutral connotations, but they are often more frightening because if we follow up on our latent possibilities there is no telling what might happen.

In practice, ego and shadow can either collaborate or tear each other apart. This is a powerful and widespread archetypal motif. It is found in the Biblical stories of Cain and Abel, Isaac and Ishmael, Jacob and Esau; in Egyptian mythology there is Horus and Set; in Christianity, Yahweh and Satan, Christ and Judas. In Freudian terminology it is known as sibling rivalry. In Jungian psychology it is called the hostile brothers motif.

One of the world's oldest surviving legends, the Gilgamesh Epic, exemplifies this motif. It illustrates not only the initial conflict between an inflated ego and an instinctual shadow—a conflict we must all come to grips with in order to have a balanced personality—but also their cooperative triumphs and what can happen when one loses the other.

The story of Gilgamesh was laboriously chiseled in stone tablets some seven thousand years ago. Briefly, it goes like this:

Gilgamesh was a young Sumerian ruler, half man and half god, who after many heroic exploits became proud and arrogant. Seeing Gilgamesh's tyranny over his subjects, the gods sent down a brother, Enkidu, to teach him a lesson. Enkidu was an animal-man. His whole body was covered with hair. At first he roamed wild on the plains, living close to nature. He was all animal until a woman dragged him into the bush and tore off his pelt. Then he became half man, familiar with lust, and

52

ravaged the countryside. Gilgamesh was angered by news of Enkidu and challenged him to do battle. Enkidu accepted and they tangled at the temple gates. It was a long and nasty struggle. They fought tooth and nail, but in the end it was a stand-off. They then embraced and toasted each other as best friends.

Together, Gilgamesh and Enkidu were half man, a quarter god and a quarter animal. For years thereafter they traveled the world righting wrongs, defeating awesome monsters like the Humbaba, guardian of the cedar forest, and the bull of heaven, a fearsome beast created by the gods to destroy Gilgamesh because he refused the seductive advances of the goddess Ishtar.

In time, Enkidu became sick and died. That was the decree of the gods, to placate Ishtar for Gilgamesh's rejection. Gilgamesh was bereft. He set out on a quest for the elixir of life. After a long journey he finally found it in the shape of a thorny plant at the bottom of the sea. Joyfully he set off for home. But one day, as he was taking a cold bath in a clear pond, a snake crept into his camp and ate the plant. Gilgamesh gnashed his teeth and wept bitterly. He had the elixir of life in hand and he lost it! Gilgamesh died a broken man.

Thus, according to the legend, snakes gained the power to shed their old skin and thereby renew their life. We humans still have to do it the hard way.

****

Brief note here, before I forget.

"Individuation does not mean losing our emotional responses, only recognizing and acknowledging when our complexes are active."

I've been asked about this by persons in long-time analysis who were hurt by someone and wondered if they were neurotic to feel that way. I said the above and counseled not to worry unless their dreams suggested otherwise.

****

The other night I watched the Coen Brothers' film *The Big Lebowski,* starring Jeff Bridges, John Goodman and Steve Buscemi. It befuddled me and I did not care for it. Tonight, responding to my film-maker son Ben's enthusiasm, I watched it again. And I turned full circle—*The Big Lebowski* is a work of genius, brilliant script and acting, impeccable direction; often goofy, but quite possibly the Coens' most creative work. Their every new film is a gem from the left field of their imaginations.

> I just dropped in,
> to see what condition
> My condition was in.....[38]

****

Now, Razr, omnivorous reader that he is, has just passed on to me this choice tidbit from *Forgotten English,* the entry for May 1, 2011:

hochle: to tumble lewdly with women in open day.—John Mactaggart's *Scottish Gallovidian Encyclopedia,* 1824.

May Day

In his *Anatomy of Abuses* (1583), Philip Stubbes wrote of a common May Day occurrence: "Men, women, and children, olde and yong... either going all togeether, or devidying themselves into companies, they goe some to the woodes and groves, some to the hilles and mountaines, some to one place, some to another, where they spende all the nighte in pleasant pastymes, and in the morning they returne, bringyng with them birchbowes, and braunches of trees, to deck their assemblies whithall." But he cautioned, "I have heard it credibly reported... by men of great gravitie, credite, and reputation, that of fourtie, threescore, or a hundred maides goyng to the woode over night, there have scarcely the thirde part of them returned home again undefiled."[39]

Not my fault, just the messenger....

---

[38] From "My Condition," lyrics by Ricky Newbury, Acuff-Rose Music, inc./ BMI – one of Lebowski's dream mantras.

[39] Jeffrey Kacirk, *Jeffrey Kacirk's Forgotten English: A 365-Day Calendar of Vanishing Vocabulary and Folklore for 2011.*

10
HAPPY TO BE A TOMATO

What is meant by "neurosis"? What marks a person as "neurotic"? The American Heritage Dictionary gives this definition of neurosis:

> Any of various functional disorders of the mind or emotions, without obvious lesion or change, and involving anxiety, phobia, or other abnormal behavior symptoms.

Not very helpful, is it? More simply put, to paraphrase Jung, neurosis is a pronounced state of disunity with oneself. We have all, at one time or another, experienced this in terms of conflicting desires.

Jung's view was that an acute outbreak of neurosis is purposeful, an opportunity to become conscious of who we are as opposed to who we think we are. By working through the symptoms that regularly accompany neurosis—anxiety, fear, depression, guilt and particularly conflict—we become aware of our limitations and discover our true strengths. Thus Jung puts a rather happy face on neurosis:

> Neurosis is really an attempt at self-cure. . . . It is an attempt of the self-regulating psychic system to restore the balance, in no way different from the function of dreams— only rather more forceful and drastic.[40]

In any breakdown in conscious functioning, energy regresses and unconscious contents are activated in an attempt to compensate the one-sidedness of consciousness:

> Neuroses, like all illnesses, are symptoms of maladjustment. Because of some obstacle—a constitutional weakness or defect, wrong education, bad experiences, an unsuitable attitude, etc.—one shrinks from the difficulties which life brings and thus finds oneself back in the world of the infant. The unconscious compensates this regression by producing symbols which, when understood objectively, that is, by means of comparative

---

[40] "The Tavistock Lectures," *The Symbolic Life,* CW 18, par. 389.

research, reactivate general ideas that underlie all such natural systems of thought. In this way a change of attitude is brought about which bridges the dissociation between man as he is and man as he ought to be.[41]

Jung called his attitude toward neurosis *energic* or final, since it was based on the potential progression of energy, rather than the Freudian view that looked for causal or mechanistic reasons for its regression. The two views are not incompatible but rather complementary: the mechanistic approach looks to the personal past for the cause of psychic discomfort in the present; Jung focused on difficulties in the present with an eye to future possibilities. Thus, instead of delving deeply into how and why one arrived at an impasse, Jung asked: "What is the necessary task which the patient will not accomplish?"[42]

Jung did not dispute Freudian theory that Oedipal fixations can manifest as neurosis in later life. He also acknowledged that certain periods in life, and particularly infancy, often have a permanent and determining influence on the personality. But he found this to be an insufficient explanation for those cases in which there was no trace of neurosis until the time of the breakdown. He wrote:

> Freud's sexual theory of neurosis is grounded on a true and factual principle. But it makes the mistake of being one-sided and exclusive; also it commits the imprudence of trying to lay hold of unconfinable Eros with the crude terminology of sex. In this respect Freud is a typical representative of the materialistic epoch, whose hope it was to solve the world riddle in a test-tube.[43]

> The psychological determination of a neurosis is only partly due to an early infantile predisposition; it must be due to some cause in the present as well. And if we carefully examine the kind of infantile fantasies and occurrences to which the neurotic is attached, we shall be obliged to agree that there is nothing in them that is specifically neurotic. Normal individuals have pretty much the same inner and outer experiences, and may be

---

[41] "The Philosophical Tree," *Alchemical Studies,* CW 13, par. 473.

[42] "Psychoanalysis and Neurosis," *Freud and Psychoanalysis,* CW 4, par. 570.

[43] "The Eros Theory," *Two Essays on Analytical Psychology,* CW 7, par. 33.

attached to them to an astonishing degree without developing a neurosis.[44]

What then determines why one person becomes neurotic while someone else, in similar circumstances, does not? Jung's answer would be that the individual psyche knows both its limits and its potential. If the former are being exceeded, or the latter not realized, a breakdown occurs. The psyche itself acts to correct the situation.

> There are vast masses of the population who, despite their notorious unconsciousness, never get anywhere near a neurosis. The few who are smitten by such a fate are really persons of the "higher" type who, for one reason or another, have remained too long on a primitive level. Their nature does not in the long run tolerate persistence in what is for them an unnatural torpor. As a result of their narrow conscious outlook and their cramped existence they save energy; bit by bit it accumulates in the unconscious and finally explodes in the form of a more or less acute neurosis.[45]

Of course, Jung's view of neurosis differs radically from the classical psychoanalytic reductive approach, but it does not substantially change what goes on in analysis. Activated fantasies still have to be brought to light, because the energy needed for life is attached to them. The object, however, is not to reveal a supposed root cause of the neurosis—its origin in infancy or early life—but to establish a connection between consciousness and the unconscious that will result in the renewed progression of energy.

The operative question in such situations is just this: "Where does your energy want to go?" The answer—not so easy to come by, and even more difficult to act upon—points the way to psychological health.

So be a tomato, potato or rhubarb, if that's what makes you happy, and don't fuss about it.

---

[44] "Psychoanalysis and Neurosis," *Freud and Psychoanalysis,* CW 4, par. 564.
[45] "The Function of the Unconscious," *Two Essays on Analytical Psychology,* CW 7, par. 291.

11
NEW HORIZONS

I saw my doctor today. She told me that all tests were super-positive, my heart strong, lungs and liver sound, kidneys ultra good.

"Doctor Sophia," I said, for that is actually her middle name, "might I live for another ten years?"

She shuffled my charts and smiled, "I don't see why not."

Well, that took me by surprise, what with my Drumming and Scotching to excess. Of course the smoking has to stop, but I persist in believing that Scotch helps to keep me alive. Of course living longer has some consequences, and I haven't figured out yet what to do in that time. Write and publish more books? Take on new clients? Romance Bo Peep to pieces? Fold my tent and sneak quietly away? I have wonderfully affectionate and attentive grown-up children and a bunch of snappy young grandkids who love to frolic in my swimming pool. Is that not enough?

I just don't know, but I won't easily give up on Eros.

Jung writes about older age in terms of the waning of the sun:

In the morning [the sun] rises from the nocturnal sea of unconsciousness and looks upon the wide, bright world which lies before it in an expanse that steadily widens the higher it climbs in the firmament. In this extension of its field of action caused by its own rising, the sun will discover its significance; it will see the attainment of the greatest possible height, and the widest possible dissemination of its blessings, as its goal. In this conviction the sun pursues its course to the unforeseen zenith—unforeseen, because its career is unique and individual, and the culminating point could not be calculated in advance. At the stroke of noon the descent begins. And the descent means the reversal of all the ideals and values that were cherished in the morning. The sun falls into contradiction with itself. It is as though it should draw in its rays instead of emitting them. Light and warmth decline and are at last extinguished. [46]

---

[46] "The Stages of Life," *The Structure and Dynamics of the Psyche,* CW 8, par. 778.

I think this is an apt and instructive metaphor that goes a long way toward explaining an older person's lack of energy for new exploits and the rigors of traveling.

Jung makes another interesting observation worth noting at length, namely that in old age the genders frequently reverse themselves:

> We might compare masculinity and femininity and their psychic components to a definite store of substances of which in the first half of life unequal use is made. A man consumes his large supply of masculine substance and has left over the small amount of feminine substance, which must now be put to use. Conversely, the woman allows her hitherto unusued supply of masculinity to become active.
>
> This change is even more noticeable in the psychic realm than in the physical. How often it happens that a man of forty-five or fifty winds up his business and the wife then dons the trousers and opens a little shop where he performs the duties of a handyman. There are many women who only awaken to social responsibility and to social consciousness after their fortieth year. In modern business life, especially in America, nervous breakdowns in the forties are a very common occurrence. If one examines the victims one finds that what has broken down is the masculine style of life which held the field up to now, and that what is leftover is an effeminate man. Contrariwise, one can observe women in these self-sale business spheres who have developed in the second half of life an uncommonly masculine tough-mindedness which thrusts the feelings and the heart aside. Very often these changes are accompanied by all sorts of catastrophes in marriage, for it is not hard to imagine what will happen when the husband discovers his tender feelings and the wife her sharpness of mind.
>
> The worst of it all is that intelligent and cultivated people live their lives without even knowing of the possibility of such transformations. [47]

---

[47] Ibid., pars. 782ff.

12
SABINA

Who was Sabina Spielrein? What was Jung's relationship with her? The answer, to steal from Oliver Stone's film *JFK* describing the mystery surrounding Kennedy's death, is "a riddle wrapped in a puzzle inside an enigma."

Fact: Sabina Spielrein (1885-1942), born in Rostov, Russia, of Russian-Jewish parents, was sent to the Burgholzli Clinic in Zurich in 1904 at the age of nineteen. She was reportedly Jung's very first patient. He diagnosed her, in accordance with Freud's views, as an hysteric. Sabina was attractive, very intelligent, and she soon became enamored of her handsome young doctor Jung, then twenty-nine and married with three children.

Jung treated Sabina for several years, as portrayed in the recent David Cronenberg movie, *A Dangerous Method* (from the book by William Kerr), where Jung is shown strapping her and perhaps against his will becoming her lover. However, we learn much more from the quasi-documentary film *My Name Was Sabina Spielrein,* purportedly based on her intimate diaries. In them she recounts her love for Jung and wish to have his child (to be called Siegfried, after Wagner's *Niebelungen).*

Jung resisted and there arose some acrimony between them, which Sabina attempted to alleviate by putting Jung in touch with Freud. There apparently ensued something of a catch-as-catch-can relationship between the three of them until 1912, when Jung finally forsook Freud's dogma to found his own school of "complex psychology." Sabina's diaries, as put out in the film *My Name Was...,,* while proclaiming her love for Jung, and assuming his for her, is not explicit about whether they were actually lovers, but it is implied.

Now, during this free-for-all, the precocious Sabina recovered her wits, managed to study for her doctorate in medicine, learn Freud's "talking cure," work with the Swiss psychiatrist Jean Piaget, and then become a psychiatrist in her own right. No small feat! In 1923, she moved back to Russia where she married and practiced with small children as a Freudian psychoanalyst until her death in the Holocaust at the age of fifty-seven.

That was indeed a tragic end for a largely unsung heroine of the early psychoanalytic movement. A lot has been written about her since the discovery of her diaries and academic articles. (Google her name for more details and references.)

What concerns me here is the attraction between Jung and Sabina, about which there can be little doubt. By 1919 Jung had found his Sophia in the young Toni Woolf (once his patient and subsequently his life-long mistress, or "second wife"). So what are we to make of this laconic, enigmatic comment by Jung in a letter to Sabina in 1919: *"Sometimes one must behave unworthily in order to survive"?*(As recounted in *My Name Was...)*

Possibly Jung wrote it in regret for his cowardice in not consummating his feelings for her, or conversely for encouraging her affection. We just don't know, because Sabina is not mentioned in any of his published writings to date (nor is Toni, for that matter).

In later years, in hindsight, the triangular relationship alerted both Jung and Freud to the dynamic of "transference," referring to a patient's intense feelings for or against the doctor, and from the other side, the "countertransference"—the doctor or analyst's feelings toward the patient/client/analysand. This dynamic is now pretty well accepted as operative in any close relationship, though it is called projection outside of a therapeutic setting.

Well, any relationship has many dimensions, from indifference to passion. In the early psychoanalytic years, little notice was taken of boundaries between doctor/therapist and patient. Nowadays, the professional therapist knows enough to at least *try* to resist an attraction, in service of the analysand's individuation. All manner of touching is currently frowned upon (even shaking hands is suspect in some Training centers), though it isn't always easy.

I have experienced this. One of my first analysands when I was training in Zurich was a voluptuous blonde (call her Helga) much like Sabina—wildly attractive and sexy, intelligent, hysterically bouncing off the walls. After a few weeks, Helga became determined to seduce me, dressing provocatively and flaunting her desire. I'm not made of stone, but I knew my ethics; I would hold her hand and ask her to calm down. Helga, a self-professed alcoholic, would storm out of our sessions saying she hated me, and then call me at all hours to apologize and declare her love. I hardly knew what to do. Once, when her husband was away, she phoned to insist I go to her. I was sorely tempted, but my better angel, or rather my brutal shadow (not the libidinous Razr), said "No." Helga finally came around to accept my position as mentor rather than lover, and eventually became conscious enough to found the first AA branch in Switzerland. Not my doing, but hers.

Well, all the foregoing is to lead up to the most incisive commentary I have ever read on the transference-countertransference phenomenon. Jung wrote a good deal on the subject, revealing his ambivalence.[48] But the late Edward F. Edinger, dean of American Jungian analysts, considered the transference, and indeed projection, to be potentially transformative. Here he is:

> Whether it occurs in analysis or in one's personal life, the transference experience is primarily a call to wholeness. The libido flows out to something that it recognizes as its own intimate possession or potentiality. This is one reason for the all-demanding possessiveness of such a relationship. Unconsciously, the individual recognizes that the analyst or friend carries a projected fragment of one's own psyche and one wants to repossess it. If one is able to assimilate the projection, one has made a decisive step toward wholeness.[49]

Edinger goes on to quote the myth recounted in Plato's *Aristophanes,* where the nature of love is discussed. In brief, Zeus decides to humble men by cutting them in half, and ever since, so the story goes, humans

---

[48] See Warren Steinberg, *Circle of Care: Clinical Issues in Jungian Therapy,* esp. pp. 9ff.
[49] "The Transference Phenomenon," in *Science of the Soul,* p. 114.

have longed to be rejoined with their other half.[50] Plato concludes with the following words that are a fitting coda to this chapter:

> Wherefore, if we would praise him who has given to us the benefit, we must praise the god *Love* who is our greatest benefactor, both leading us in this life back to our own nature, and giving us high hopes for the future, for he promises that if we are pious, he will restore us to our original state, and heal us and make us happy and blessed.[51]

---

[50] *The Dialogues of Plato,* pp. 316ff.
[51] Ibid., p. 318.

13
INTIMACY WITH DISTANCE

When a person complains that he is always on bad terms with his wife or
the people he loves, and that there are terrible scenes
or resistances between them, you will see when you analyze this person
that he has an attack of hatred. He has been living in
participation mystique *with those he loves. He has spread himself over*
other people until he has become identical with them, which is a violation
of the principle of individuality. Then they have
resistances naturally, in order to keep themselves apart.[52]

One of the greatest single obstacles to a mature relationship is the ideal
of togetherness. It is an ideal based on the archetypal motif of wholeness.
Find your soul mate, your other half, and you'll live happily ever after.
This is a very old idea. You find it in Greek philosophy, for instance in
Plato's *Symposium,* where Aristophanes pictures humans as originally
whole but arrogant.[53] As punishment, already noted here, Zeus cut them
in half, and now, it is said, we forever seek to replace our lost other.[54]

There is nothing intrinsically wrong with this ideal. The mistake is in
expecting to find our "lost other" in the outside world. In fact, it is our
contrasexual inner other, animus or anima, who is more properly the object of our search. Outer relationships, already hampered by personal
complexes and a multitude of day-to-day concerns, cannot bear the extra
weight of archetypal expectations. Although individuation is not possible
without relationship, it is not compatible with togetherness.

After the passage quoted above, Jung continues:

---

[52] *The Psychology of Kundalini Yoga: Notes of the Seminar Given in 1932 by C.G. Jung,*
p. 7.

[53] *Symposium,* 14-16 (189A-193E).

[54] See esp. James Hollis, *The Eden Project: In Search of the Magical Other,* for a valu-
able explication of this theme.

I say, "Of course it is most regrettable that you always get into trouble, but don't you see what you are doing? You love somebody, you identify with them, and of course you prevail against the objects of your love and repress them by your very self-evident identity. You handle them as if they were yourself, and naturally there will be resistances. It is a violation of the individuality of those people, and it is a sin against your own individuality. Those resistances are a most useful and important instinct: you have resistances, scenes, and disappointments so that you may become finally conscious of yourself, and then hatred is no more."[55]

Individuation, finding your own unique path, requires a focus on the inner axis, ego to unconscious—getting to know yourself. The ideal of togetherness lets you off that hook. Togetherness doesn't acknowledge the natural boundaries between people, and it gives short shrift to their differences. All you're left with is unconscious identity. When you are on the path of individuation, focused on your own psychological development, you relate to others from a position of personal integrity. This is the basis for intimacy with distance. It is not as sentimental as togetherness, but it's not as sticky either.

A relationship based on intimacy with distance does not require separate living quarters. Intimacy with distance means *psychological* separation, which comes about through the process of differentiation—knowing where you end and the other begins. Intimacy with distance can be as close and as warm as you want, and it's psychologically clean. Togetherness is simply fusion, the submersion of two individualities into one, variously called symbiosis, identification, *participation mystique*. It can feel good for a while but in the long run it does not work.

Togetherness is to intimacy with distance as being in love is to loving. When you're in love, you absolutely need the other. This is symptomatic of bonding, which is natural between parent and infant, and also at the beginning of any relationship at any age. But need, finally, is not compatible with loving; it only shows the degree to which one lacks personal resources. Better take your need to a therapist than dump it on the one you love. Need in an intimate relationship easily becomes the rationale

---

[55] *The Psychology of Kundalini Yoga*, p. 7.

for power, leading to the fear of loss on one hand, and resentment on the other.

The key to intimacy with distance is the self-containment of each of the partners, which in turn depends on how much they know about themselves. When you are self-contained, psychologically independent, you don't look to another person for completion. You don't identify with others and you're not victimized by their projections. You know where you stand and you live by your personal truth—come what may. You can survive cold shoulders and you can take the heat.

When you are self-contained, you have your own sacred space, your own *temenos*. You might invite someone in, but you're not driven to, and you don't feel abandoned if the invitation is declined. You respect the loved ones' boundaries, their freedom and privacy, even their secrets; you give them space and you don't knowingly push their buttons. You don't judge and you don't blame. There is interest in, and empathy for, the concerns of others, but you don't take them on as your own.

When you are psychologically separate, not identified with your mate, you don't need the other to agree with you and you don't need to be right. You don't expect the other to change in order to suit your needs, and you don't ask it of yourself either. And if over time you can't accept the other but still can't leave, well, that is the stuff of analysis: conflict and complexes.

The bond between two people is a precious and mysterious thing, not entirely explained by the theory of complexes and the phenomenon of projection. But this much at least is true: there is an optimum distance in every relationship that evolves through trial and error and good will—if you know who you are and can stop pressing for more than you get.

14
EMERSON & ETCETERA

"What are you doing, Zek?" said Judge Webster to his eldest boy.
"Nothing."
"What are you doing, Daniel?"
"Helping Zek."
A tolerably correct account of most of our activity today.
—Ralph Waldo Emerson, Journal entry, 1841.

Ralph Waldo Emerson (1804-1882) is not well known these days, but in the 1800s he was a giant—poet, essayist, philosopher, and sometimes a Unitarian/Universalist minister, dominating the field of belles lettres for half a century. He was a wry, acerbic observer of the human condition and the political turmoil of his time. When he died he was one of the most famous intellectuals in America.

Edward F. Edinger was a great admirer of Emerson. He writes:

I think Lincoln and Emerson are the finest products of America. They're what make me proud to be an American..... [Emerson is] the harbinger of Jungian psychology in America. [The late Jungian analyst] Joe Henderson told me in a personal conversation that Jung said to him, "If you understand Emerson, you'll understand my psychology." Jung refers to Emerson a number of times in the *Collected Works* [though never at any length].... The insights that reside in Emerson's writings are just remarkable in the light of twentieth-century psychology.[56]

Emerson's journals were his life's work, which he kept assiduously from the age of sixteen until he was seventy-eight. They were the starting point for virtually everything in his celebrated essays, lectures and

---

[56] "The Psyche in Culture," in George R. Elder and Dianne D. Cordic, eds., *An American Jungian: In Honor of Edward F. Edinger,* pp. 57f.

poems—a "savings bank" in which his insights began to cohere and yield interest—both a commonplace book where he recorded the choicest of the days' anecdotes, ideas and phrases from his voracious and wide-ranging reading and a fascinating diary in the ordinary sense of the term. It would be a hundred years after his death before these intimate records would appear in print in their entirety.

I have been immersing myself in Emerson's *Journals* now for several days. They are pure Eros. He does not expostulate on abstract ideas. On almost every page there is a pithy rebuke of a jackass politician, a poetic comment on his neighbor's horse, or a witty put-down of a lauded literary figure of the day, all at once both earthy and sublime. Emerson is a splendid writer! He doesn't debate and never argues a point. Words flow from his quill like honey from a hive, sweet and substantial, never to decay. Listen to this snippet:

> Love is temporary & ends with marriage. Marriage is the perfection which love aimed at, ignorant of what it sought. Marriage is a good known only to the parties. A relation of perfect understanding, aid, contentment, possession of themselves & of the world,—which dwarfs love to green fruit.[57]

See the two-edged sword in that passage!—love doesn't last, and/or morphs into something much more precious (well, at least in Emerson's own short-cut union with the love of his life, Margaret Fuller, who drowned untimely while swimming in Brazil, leaving him with son Waldo and daughter Edith).

****

Sorry folks, but I hit a road block. There are so many Emerson passages I could quote that I'm struck dumb. I may come back to him, but meanwhile in my eclectic turret I find myself back where I started this book, celebrating the beloved songwriter and singer-pianist Hoagy Carmichael (1899-1981), who wrote so many memorable tunes, like "Stardust," "Georgia on My Mind," and "The Nearness of You." He was a self-professed "jazz maniac." When his mother heard him tinkling on their

---

[57] *Emerson: Selected Journals, 1841-1877,* p. 499.

golden oak piano, she admonished him: "Music is fun, Hoagland, but it don't buy you cornpone."

Well, young Hoagy went on to buy more cornpone than anyone in his birth state of Indiana ever knew existed. Does this bring back memories?:

And now the purple dusk of twilight time
Steals across the meadows of my heart
High up in the sky the little stars climb
Always reminding me that we're apart

You wander down the lane and far away
Leaving me a song that will not die
Love is now the stardust of yesterday
The music of the years gone by

Sometimes I wonder why I spend
The lonely night dreaming of a song
The melody haunts my reverie
And I am once again with you
When our love was new
And each kiss an inspiration
But that was long ago
Now my consolation
Is in the stardust of a song

Beside a garden wall
When stars are bright
You are in my arms
The nightingale tells his fairy tale
of paradise where roses grew
Though I dream in vain
In my heart it always will remain
My stardust melody
The memory of love's refrain.[58]

For decades from the 1920s, Hoagy was the greatest of the great. And then along came Muddy Waters, Chuck Berry, Elvis, Sinatra, the Rolling Stones and the Beatles (to name but a few), and the sound of music was

---

[58] "Stardust," music by Carmichael, these lyrics by Nat King Cole; Ascap.

changed forever. Now we have rap and hip-hop and who knows what else, but Hoagy's tunes have survived through all the changes.

Dance with the one who brung you.

****

Okay, moving right along to gravitas, here are other choice nuggets from Emerson's *Journals:*

> No man can write anything who does not think that what he writes is for the time the history of the world, or do anything well who does not suppose his work to be of greatest importance. My work may be of none but I must not think it of none or I shall not do it with impunity. Woso does what he thinks mean, is mean.[59]

And this:

> Jesus said, "When he looketh on her, he hath already committed adultery". But he is an adulterer already, *before yet he has looked on the woman,* by the superfluity of animal, & the weakness of thought, in his constitution. Who meets him, or who meets her, in the street, sees at once, they are ripe to be each other's victim.[60]

And get a load of this cogent, spirited observation:

> In feeble individuals, the sex & the digestion are all, absorb the entire vitality; and, the stronger these are, one would say, the individual is only so much the weaker. Of course, the more of these drones perish, the better for the hive. Later, perhaps they give birth, to some superior individual who has sufficient force to add to this animal a new aim, & an apparatus of means to work it out. Instantly all the ancestors become guano [shit]. Thus most men are mere bulls & most women cows; with however now & then an individual who has an Aeolian attachment or an additional cell opened in his brain as an architectural or a musical or a philological knack; some stray taste or talent, as, a love of flowers, or of chemistry, or pigments, or a narrative talent, a good hand for chess, or a good foot for dancing, &c.—which skill nowise alters the life of himself or the people,

---

[59] *Emerson: Selected Journals 1841-1877,* p. 29.
[60] Ibid., p. 564. [Think puer/puella.]

nowise alters their rank in the scale of nature, but merely serves to pass the time,—the bulling and milking going on as before.[61]

And this pithy comment:

Not to be appreciated by one we dearly love,—yes, that would be inconvenient & must at last reduce the flame.[62]

****

Now, while I'm at it, I cannot resist expressing my appreciation of the romantic, sometimes-monk and always-singer/poet Leonard Cohen, born in 1934 in Montreal, Quebec, celebrated around the world for his sensuous way with words. Here is a choice example from his latest collection, *Book of Longing:*

Thousand Kisses Deep
for Sandy 1945-1998

You came to me this morning
And you handled me like meat
You'd have to be a man to know
How good that feels how sweet
My mirror twin my next of kin
I'd know you in my sleep
And who but you would take me in
A thousand kisses deep

I loved you when you opened
Like a lily to the heat
I'm just another snowman
Standing in the rain and sleet
Who loved you with his frozen love
His second-hand physique
With all he is and all he was
A thousand kisses deep

I know you had to lie to me

---

61 Ibid., p. 550.
62 Ibid., p. 28.

I know you had to cheat
To pose all hot and high behind
The veils of sheer deceit
Our perfect porn aristocrat
So elegant and cheap
I'm old but I'm still into that
A thousand kisses deep

And I'm still working with the wine
Still dancing cheek to cheek
The band is playing Auld Lang Syne
The heart will not retreat
I ran with Diz and Danté
I never had their sweep
But once or twice they let me lay
A thousand kisses deep

. . . .

I'm good at love I'm good at hate
It's in between I freeze
Been working out but it's too late
It's been too late for years
But you look fine you really do
The pride of Boogie Street
Somebody must have died for you
A thousand kisses deep

. . . .

Confined to sex we pressed against
The limits of the sea
I saw there were no oceans left
For scavengers like me
I made it to the forward deck
I blessed our remnant fleet
And then consented to be wrecked
A thousand kisses deep

I'm turning tricks, I'm getting fixed
I'm back on Boogie Street
I guess they won't exchange the gifts

That you were meant to keep
And sometimes when the night is slow
The wretched and the meek
We gather up our hearts and go
A thousand kisses deep

And fragrant is the thought of you
The file on you complete
Except what we forgot to do
A thousand kisses deep[63]

****

And Emerson again:

There is one mind common to all individual men. Every man is an inlet to
the same and to all of the same. He that is once admitted to the right of
reason is made a freeman of the whole estate. What Plato has thought, he
may think; what a saint has felt, he may feel; what at any time has befallen
any man, he can understand. Who hath access to this universal mind is a
party to all that is or can be done, for this is the only and sovereign
agent.[64]

---

[63] Leonard Cohen, "Thousand Kisses Deep" (condensed) , in *Book of Longing,* pp. 56f.
[64] "History," in *Essays: First and Second Series,* p. 7.

15
SOLITUDE, LONELINESS
& CONSCIOUSNESS

Since Freud's day, and, more particularly, since the emergence of the ob-
ject-relations school of psycho-analysis, there has been a shift of emphasis
in understanding and interpreting transference. The majority of psycho-
analysts, social workers, and other members of the so-called "helping professions" consider that intimate personal relationships are the chief source
of human happiness. Conversely, it is widely assumed that those who do
not enjoy the satisfactions provided by such relationships are neurotic,
immature, or in some other way abnormal. Today, the thrust of most forms
of psychotherapy, whether with individuals or groups, is directed toward
understanding what has gone wrong with the patient's relationships with
significant persons in his or her past, in order that the patient can be helped
toward making more fruitful and fulfilling human relationships in the future.

—Anthony Storr, *Solitude.*

Living alone doesn't necessarily mean being lonely, though from time to
time the two may go together. It is in the nature of the psyche that those
who choose to live a solitary life should occasionally long for the company of others, and vice versa. ("Let my shadow live!" cries the introvert; "Please, no more parties," pleads the extravert.)

Being alone seems to facilitate creativity. Writers, poets, musicians,
artists of any kind, for example, need endless time on their own in order
to incubate their nascent ideas. This may perturb their friends and partners, but it goes with the territory, so to speak. One cannot create in a
crowd. Indeed, the company of others seems to be anathema to the act of
creation. For example, the eminent British psychiatrist Anthony Storr
writes of the artist's response to a depressed mood:

Creative people are used to solitude.... Instead of seeking friends in whom

74

to confide, or counselors to whom to tell their troubles, they use their gifts to come to terms with, and to make sense of, their sufferings. Once a work is completed, it can be shared with others; but the initial response to depression is to turn inward rather than outward.[65]

Later Storr adds:

Although man is a social being, who certainly needs interaction with others, there is considerably variation in the depth of the relationships which individuals form with each other. All human beings need interests as well as relationships; all are geared toward the impersonal as well as the personal. The events of early childhood, inherited gifts and capacities, temperamental differences, and a host of other factors may influence whether individuals turn predominantly toward others or toward solitude to find the meaning of their lives.[66]

Enter Jung, who links the feeling of loneliness to an increase in consciousness:

Genesis represents the act of becoming conscious as a taboo infringement, as though knowledge meant that a sacrosanct barrier had been impiously overstepped. I think that Genesis is right in so far as every step towards greater consciousness is a kind of Promethean guilt: through knowledge, the gods are as it were robbed of their fire, that is, something that was the property of the unconscious powers is torn out of its natural context and subordinated to the whims of the conscious mind. The man who has usurped the new knowledge suffers, however, a transformation or enlargement of consciousness which no longer resembles that of his fellow men.[67]

Elsewhere, in a similar vein, discussing the psychology of child-figures appearing in dreams, Jung writes:

Higher consciousness, or knowledge going beyond our present-day consciousness, is equivalent to being *all alone in the world.* This loneliness

---

[65] Anthony Storr, *Solitude,* p. 129.

[66] Ibid., pp. 201f.

[67] "The Persona As a Segment of the Collective Psyche," *Two Essays on Analytical Psychology,* CW 7, par. 243n.

75

expresses the conflict between the bearer or symbol of higher consciousness and his surroundings.[68]

****

Being alone is relatively easy for introverts. They may lack a vital, ongoing connection with the outer world but they generally have an active inner life. Extraverts are used to hustle and bustle and find it more difficult to live with just themselves. But whatever one's typology, the great challenge in the development of personality is to find a personal center. Elsewhere in this book I have spoken of the need for a personal container, but they come to the same thing.

Initially one's center is projected onto the immediate family, a self-contained unit experienced as wholeness. Without a family, whether nurturing or repressive, we are apt to feel rootless, at loose ends. The loss of such a container is clearly at work behind the emotional distress of orphans or a child whose parents split up, but that same motif is also constellated in grown-ups when one ascribes to values other than those sanctioned by the collective, or when any close relationship breaks up.

Loneliness feels like one has been abandoned. Mythologically, abandonment is associated with the childhood experience of gods and divine heroes—Zeus, Dionysus, Poseidon, Moses, Romulus and Remus, and so on. In fact, the motif is so widespread that Jung describes abandonment as "a necessary condition and not just a concomitant symptom," of the potentially higher consciousness symbolized by images of the child in a person's dreams.[69]

Anyone in the process of becoming independent must detach from his or her origins: mother, family, society. Sometimes this transition happens smoothly. If it does not, the result is twofold: the "poor me" syndrome, characteristic of the regressive longing for dependence, and a psychic experience of a potentially creative nature—the positive side of the

---

[68] "The Psychology of the Child Archetype," *The Archetypes and the Collective Unconscious,* CW 9i, par. 288.

[69] "The Psychology of the Child Archetype," *The Archetypes and the Collective Unconscious,* CW 9i, par. 287.

divine child archetype: new life, exciting new possibilities. The incompatibility between these two directions generates a conflict that may precipitate a psychological crisis. The conflict is the price that has to be paid in order to grow up. On the one hand, we long to return to the past; on the other, we are drawn inexorably toward an unknown future.

Initially, this conflict goes hand in hand with the feeling of loneliness, behind which is the archetypal motif of the abandoned child. Thus Jung observes, "Higher consciousness . . . is equivalent to being *all alone in the world.*"[70] In short, individuation and personality are gifts that are paid for dearly. Thus Jung writes:

> The development of personality . . . is at once a charisma and a curse, because its first fruit is the segregation of the single individual from the undifferentiated and unconscious herd. This means isolation, and there is no more comforting word for it. Neither family nor society nor position can save one from this fate, nor yet the most successful adaptation to the environment.[71]

****

The antidote to the feeling of loneliness, of abandonment, is the development of personality. But this does not happen unless one chooses his or her own way consciously and with moral deliberation. And you can make a commitment to go your own way only if you believe that way to be better for you than conventional ways of a moral, social, political or religious nature—any of the well-known "isms." Those who adhere to them do not choose their own way; they develop not themselves but a method and a collective mode of life at the cost of their own wholeness.

Personality is not the prerogative of genius, nor is mental prowess a significant factor in individuation. Just as in fairy tales, where so many psychic patterns are illustrated, the one who finds the "treasure hard to attain" is often as not a Dummling, an innocent fool who follows his instincts.

---

[70] Ibid., par. 288.
[71] "The Development of Personality," *The Development of Personality,* CW 17, pars. 293f.

77

****

Now, let the Beatles have a few words here, though not particularly happy ones:

> Ah, look at all the lonely people
> Ah, look at all the lonely people
> Eleanor Rigby, picks up the rice
> In the church where a wedding has been
>
> Lives in a dream
> Waits at the window, wearing the face
> That she keeps in a jar by the door
> Who is it for?
>
> All the lonely people
> Where do they all come from?
> All the lonely people
> Where do they all belong?
>
> Father McKenzie, writing the words
> of a sermon that no one will hear
> No one comes near
>
> Look at him working, darning his socks
> In the night when there's nobody there
> What does he care?
>
> All the lonely people
> Where do they all come from?
> All the lonely people
> Where do they all belong?
>
> Ah, look at all the lonely people
> Ah, look at all the lonely people
>
> Eleanor Rigby, died in the church
> And was buried along with her name
> Nobody came
>
> Father McKenzie, wiping the dirt
> From his hands as he walks from the grave
> No one was saved
>
> All the lonely people

78

(Ah, look at all the lonely people)
Where do they all come from?
All the lonely people
(Ah, look at all the lonely people)
Where do they all belong?[72]

****

Okay, the above is rather a lot to digest, so let's clear our heads with a hopeful song by the inimitable Cat Stevens before he morphed into the bland Yousef Islam:

Well I left my happy home to see what I could find out
I left my folk and friends with the aim to clear my mind out
Well I hit the rowdy road and many kinds I met there
Many stories told me of the way to get there

So on and on I go, the seconds tick the time out
There's so much left to know, and I'm on the road to find out

Well in the end I'll know, but on the way I wonder
Through descending snow, and through the frost and thunder

Well, I listen to the wind come howl, telling me I have to hurry
I listen to the robin's song saying not to worry

So on and on I go, the seconds tick the time out
There's so much left to know, and I'm on the road to find out

Then I found myself alone, hopin' someone would miss me
Thinking about my home, and the last woman to kiss me, kiss me

But sometimes you have to moan when nothing seems to suit yer
But nevertheless you know you're locked towards the future

So on and on you go, the seconds tick the time out
There's so much left to know, and I'm on the road to find out

Then I found my head one day when I wasn't even trying

---

[72] "Eleanor Rigby," on *Rubber Soul;* Ascap.

And here I have to say, 'cause there is no use in lying, lying

Yes the answer lies within, so why not take a look now?
Kick out the devil's sin, pick up, pick up the good book now.[73]

****

And Emerson again:

> What I must do is all that concerns me, not what the people think. This
> rule, equally arduous in actual and in intellectual life, may serve for the
> whole distinction between greatness and meanness. It is the harder, be-
> cause you will always find those who think they know what is your duty
> better than you know it. It is easy in the world to live after the world's
> opinion; it is easy in solitude to live after our own; but the great man is he
> who in the midst of the crowd keeps with perfect sweetness the independ-
> ence of solitude.[74]

---

[73] "On the Road To Find Out," on *Tea For The Tillerman"*; Ascap.
[74] *Essays: First and Second Series,* p. 33.

16
THE VALUE OF CONFLICT

*If a man faced with a conflict of duties undertakes to deal
with them absolutely on his own responsibility, and
before a judge who sits in judgment on him day and night,
he may well find himself in an isolated position. There is now
an authentic secret in his life which cannot be discussed—
if only because he is involved in an endless inner trial in which
he is his own counsel and ruthless examiner.*[75]

Any conflict situation constellates the problem of opposites. Broadly speaking, "the opposites" refers to ego-consciousness and the unconscious. This is true whether the conflict is recognized as an internal one or not, since conflicts with other people are almost always externalizations of an unconscious conflict within oneself. Because they are not made conscious, they are acted out on others through projection.

Whatever the conscious attitude may be, the opposite is in the unconscious. There is no way to haul this out by force. If we try, it will refuse to come. That is why the process of analysis is seldom productive unless there is an active conflict. Indeed, as long as outer life proceeds relatively smoothly, there is no need to deal with the unconscious. But when we are troubled, it is wise to take it into consideration, for instance by attending to dreams.

The classic conflict situation is one in which there is the possibility of, or temptation to, more than one course of action. Theoretically the options may be many, but in practice a conflict is usually between two, each carrying its own chain of consequences. In such cases the psychological reality is that two separate personalities are involved. It is helpful to think of these as different aspects of oneself; in other words, as personifications of complexes.

Perhaps the most painful conflicts are those involving duty or a choice

---

[75] Jung, *Memories, Dreams, Reflections,* p. 345.

between security and freedom. Such conflicts generate a great deal of inner tension. As long as they are not conscious, the tension manifests as physical symptoms, particularly in the stomach, the back and the neck. Conscious conflict, on the other hand, is experienced as moral or ethical tension.

I have worked analytically with married men and women who had secret lovers and troubling physical ailments. By and large, they did not come to me because of a conflict over their extramarital activities, which were safely compartmentalized. In truth, they were split and didn't know it. But when their right hand (ego) openly acknowledged what their left hand (shadow) was doing, their physical symptoms disappeared. There then followed moral tension and a conscious search for resolution.

Conflict is a hallmark of neurosis, but conflict is not invariably neurotic. Life naturally involves the collision between conflicting obligations and incompatible desires. Some degree of conflict is even desirable, since without it the flow of life is sluggish. Conflict only becomes neurotic when it settles in and interferes, physically or mentally, with the way one functions.

Two preliminary possibilities exist for resolving a conflict. You can tally up the pros and cons on each side and reach a logically satisfying decision, or you can opt for what you "really want," then proceed to do what is necessary to make it possible.

Many minor conflicts can be decided by reason. But serious conflicts do not so easily disappear; in fact they often arise precisely because of a one-sided rational attitude, and thus are more likely to be prolonged than solved by reason alone.

Where this is so, it is appropriate to ask, "But what do *I* want?" or alternatively, "What do I *want?*" These are useful questions, for the first, with the accent on "I," clarifies the individual ego position (as opposed to what others might want), and the second, stressing "want," activates the feeling function (judgment, evaluation).

A serious conflict usually involves a disparity between thinking and feeling. If feeling is not a conscious factor in the conflict, it needs to be introduced; the same may be said for thinking.

If the ego position coincides with, or can accept, the feeling attitude, all well and good. But if these are not compatible and the ego refuses to give way, then the situation remains at an impasse. That is the clinical picture of neurotic conflict, the resolution of which requires a dialogue with one's other sides. We can learn a good deal about ourselves through relationships with others, but the unconscious is a more objective mirror of who we really are.

Jung believed that the potential resolution of a conflict is activated by holding the tension between the opposites. When every motive has an equally strong counter motive—that is, when the conflict between the ego and the unconscious is at its peak—there is a damming up of vital energy. But life cannot tolerate a standstill. If the ego can hold the tension, something quite unexpected emerges, an irrational "third" that effectively resolves the situation.

This irrational "third" is what Jung called the transcendent function, which typically manifests as a symbol. Here is how he describes the process:

> [A conflict] requires a real solution and necessitates a third thing in which the opposites can unite. Here the logic of the intellect usually fails, for in a logical antithesis there is no third. The "solvent" can only be of an irrational nature. In nature the resolution of opposites is always an energic process: she acts *symbolically* in the truest sense of the word, doing something that expresses both sides, just as a waterfall visibly mediates between above and below.[76]

Outer circumstances may remain the same, but a change takes place in the individual. This generally appears as a new attitude toward oneself and others; energy previously locked up in a state of indecision is released and once again it becomes possible to move forward.

At that point, it is as if you were to stand on a mountain top watching a raging storm below—the storm may go on, but you are outside of it, to some extent objective, no longer emotionally stressed. There is a sense of peace. This is not essentially different from the traditional Christian con-

---

[76] "The Conjunction," *Mysterium Coniunctionis,* CW 14, par. 705.

cept of grace—"the peace that passeth all understanding"—except that it doesn't come from a distant God; it wells up inside.

This process requires patience and an ego strong enough to bend but not break, otherwise a decision will be made out of desperation, just to escape the tension. But when a decision is made prematurely—when the tension has not been held long enough—then the other side, the option that was not chosen, will be constellated even more strongly and we're right back in the fire.

Ah, one asks, but aren't some conflicts intrinsically insoluble?

Well, yes, that may be true in terms of external solutions. But a solution in outer life is as often as not simply avoiding or rationalizing the underlying problem. As Jung writes:

> If a man cannot get on with his wife, he naturally thinks the conflict would be solved if he married someone else. When such marriages are examined they are seen to be no solution at all. The old Adam enters upon the new marriage and bungles it just as badly as he did the earlier one. A real solution comes only from within, and then only because the patient has been brought to a different attitude.[77]

Jung, as a man of his time, was not gender-conscious. If he were writing the above today, I dare say he would have reworded it to include women, putting Eve on the hot seat along with Adam.

---

[77] "Some Crucial Points in Psychoanalysis: A Correspondence between Dr. Jung and Dr. Loÿ," *Freud and Psychoanalysis,* CW 4, par. 606.

17
GROWING UPSIDE DOWN

I want to go to bed, but I am held back by my obsession with writing, mine and that of other people. I read a lot and learn from other writers. Sometimes I steal a phrase or two from them, as do they from me. Well, that's been going on since Gutenberg invented the printing press in 1450. But mostly I plagiarize my own writing if it seems appropriate, thinking that, after all, I can't assume readers are familiar with my other books. And I think it's fair to present earlier thoughts in a new context.

I am only happy when I'm reading, writing or making love. That's the actual truth of it, not forgetting my libidinous side-kick Razr, The Beatles' "Nowhere Man" haunted me for years. I wrote a play around it when I was twenty-five; it just went into the unpublishable heap of juvenilia that accumulated in the pleroma over the years. A propos, my son Dave has just turned fifty-one, and I got to thinking that at his age I first became aware of who I was, my individuality, and then went on to write and publish many more books. I am not famous, but I am prolific. I became a "somewhere man," so to speak, at least to myself. This experience gives me hope for others in my analytic care.

Okay, so these lyrics used to hurt like hell (call it being complexed):

He's a real Nowhere Man
Sitting in his Nowhere Land
Making all his nowhere plans for nobody

Doesn't have a point of view
Knows not where he's going to
Isn't he a bit like you and me?

Nowhere Man, please listen
You don't know what you're missing
Nowhere Man, the world is at your command

He's as blind as he can be
Just sees what he wants to see

Nowhere Man, can you see me at all?

Nowhere Man, don't worry
Take your time, don't hurry
Leave it all 'til somebody else lends you a hand

Doesn't have a point of view
Knows not where he's going to
Isn't he a bit like you and me?

Nowhere Man, please listen
You don't know what you're missing
Nowhere Man, the world is at your command

He's a real Nowhere Man
Sitting in his Nowhere Land
Making all his nowhere plans for nobody
Making all his nowhere plans for nobody
Making all his nowhere plans for nobody.

As far as I can see, the writer's lot is generally not a happy one. You can read the biographies for yourself: F. Scott Fitzgerald, Franz Kafka, John Steinbeck, Mark Twain, Ernest Hemingway, you name them, all haunted men unable to love, or feeling inadequate and overcome by alcohol or other drugs. And their female counterparts—especially poets—fare no better. Writing is a vocation bound to break your heart if you let it be your reason for living. Rather see it as an adjunct to the other loves in your life, like family and the work you do to pay for vegetables.

Stay sane; bend but don't break. Or, as the wise old craftsman Gepetto tells Pinocchio in a little-known version of the story, "Stay wood. There are lots of real boys. Stay wood and act real."

****

Have you noticed, as you get older, that everyone you meet, or see on the street, reminds you of someone you know or a movie actor? Look, there goes Al Pacino, Robert Redford, Christopher Plummer, Dustin Hoffman, Cameron Diaz, Julia Roberts, your Grade Six teacher, Ollie from the gym, Sieux City Sue, Mahalia Jackson; there's your Jasmine and Rebecca, and so on, each visage as much of an illusion as the reality.

86

****

She sat on my lap and unbuckled my belt. Then I lost consciousness until a day or two later, can't keep track of time anymore. But I came to my senses feeling real happy.

A man's vilest mood may be undone by the tender love of a good woman. And a sorrowful woman who has been wronged? She too relinquishes her hurt under the ministrations of a loved one.

Long live Eros.—*Razr.*

****

So now, before turning the lights out, let's hear from Ol' Blue Eyes on the pitfalls and aftermath of love:

> It's a quarter to three,
> There's no one in the place 'cept you and me
> So set em up Joe
> I got a little story I think you oughtta know
>
> We're drinking my friend
> To the end of a brief episode
> So make it one for my baby
> And one more for the road
>
> I know the routine
> Put another nickel in that there machine
> I'm feeling so bad
> Won't you make the music easy and sad
>
> I could tell you a lot
> But you gotta to be true to your code
> So make it one for my baby
> And one more for the road
>
> You'd never know it
> But buddy I'm a kind of poet
> And I've got a lot of things I wanna say
> And if I'm gloomy, please listen to me
> Till it's all, all talked away
>
> Well, that's how it goes

And Joe I know you're getting' anxious to close
So thanks for the cheer
I hope you didn't mind
My bending your ear

But this torch that I found
It's gotta be drowned
Or it soon might explode
So make it one for my baby
And one more for the road.[78]

Talk about sad—but Sinatra was a master at making sad, soulful lyrics sound hopeful and upbeat. It is said that he conspired with gangsters to further his rise to fame. Well, so what, who wouldn't? I am envious because I've had no offers.

So I go about my business in my turret, in relative obscurity. This has its own satisfaction, thanks very much.

Just saying.

****

And Emerson, a propos:

The soul is no traveller; the wise man stays at home, and when his neccessities, his duties, on any occasion call him from his house, or into foreign lands, he is at home still, and shall make men sensible by the expression of his countenance, that he goes the missionary of wisdom and virtue, and visits cities and men like a sovereign, and not like an interloper or a valet.[79]

---

[78] Frank Sinatra, "One More For the Road," written by Johnny Mercer and Harold Arlen; Ascap.

[79] "Self-Reliance,"in *Essays, First and Second Series,* p. 47.

18

A PSYCHOLOGICAL COMPASS

The four functions are somewhat like the four points of the compass; they are just as arbitrary and just as indispensable. . . . But one thing I must confess: I would not for anything dispense with this compass on my psychological voyages of discovery.[80]

Why do we move through life the way we do? Why are we better at some activities than others? Why do some of us prefer to be alone rather than with other people—or at a party instead of reading a book? Why don't we all function in the same way?

From earliest times, attempts have been made to categorize individual attitudes and behavior patterns in order to explain the differences between people. Jung's model of typology is one of them. It is the basis for modern "tests" such as the Myers-Briggs Type Indicator (MBTI), used by corporations and institutions in order to classify a person's interests, attitudes and behavior patterns, and hence the type of work or education they might be best suited for.

Jung did not develop his model of psychological types for this purpose. Rather than label people as this or that type, he sought simply to explain the differences between the ways we function and interact with our surroundings in order to promote a better understanding of human psychology in general, and one's own way of seeing the world in particular.

After many years of research, Jung identified eight typological groups: two personality attitudes—*introversion* and *extraversion*—and four functions—*thinking, sensation, intuition* and *feeling,* each of which may operate in an introverted or extraverted way.

In Jung's model, introversion and extraversion are psychological

---

[80] "A Psychological Theory of Types," *Psychological Types,* CW 6, pars. 958f.

modes of adaptation. In the former, the movement of energy is toward the inner world. In the latter, interest is directed toward the outer world. In one case the subject (inner reality) and in the other the object (outer reality) is of primary importance. Whether one is predominately introverted or extraverted—as opposed to what one is doing at any particular time—depends on the direction one's energy naturally, and usually, flows.[81] It follows, then, that the opposite function is in the unconscious.

Each of the four functions has its special area of expertise. *Thinking* refers to the process of cognitive thought; *sensation* is perception by means of the physical sense organs; *feeling* is the function of subjective judgment or valuation; and *intuition* refers to perception via the unconscious.

Briefly, the sensation function establishes that something exists, thinking tells us what it means, feeling tells us what it's worth to us, and through intuition we have a sense of what can be done with it (the possibilities).

No one function by itself (and neither attitude alone) is sufficient for ordering our experience of ourselves or the world around us:

> For complete orientation all four functions should contribute equally: thinking should facilitate cognition and judgment, feeling should tell us how and to what extent a thing is important or unimportant for us, sensation should convey concrete reality to us through seeing, hearing, tasting, etc., and intuition should enable us to divine the hidden possibilities in the background, since these too belong to the complete picture of a given situation.[82]

---

[81] Note that introversion is quite different from introspection, which refers to self-examination. Although introverts may have more time or inclination for introspection, introverts have no monopoly on psychological awareness. It might be noted here that introversion is not highly valued in Western culture, and little understood; viz. the rumor that the upcoming DSM5 (*Diagnostic and Statistical Manual of Psychiatric Disorders*, 2013) will dub introversion as a pathological symptom.

[82] Ibid., par. 900. Jung acknowledged that the four orienting functions do not contain everything in the conscious psyche. Will power and memory, for instance, are not included in his model, because although they may be affected by the way one functions typologically, they are not in themselves typological determinants.

In everyday usage, the feeling function is often confused with an emotional reaction. Emotion, more properly called affect, is invariably the result of an activated complex, which is accompanied by noticeable physical symptoms. When not contaminated by a complex, feeling can in fact be quite cold.

Jung's basic model, including the relationship between the four functions, is a quaternity. In the following diagram, thinking is arbitrarily placed at the top; any of the other functions might be put there, according to which one a person most favors.

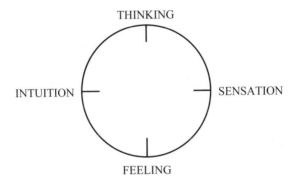

THINKING

INTUITION   SENSATION

FEELING

Typologically, opposites can attract or repel. Hence it is common for someone with a dominant thinking function, for instance, to be attracted to a feeling type—or shun such a person because of his or her very differentness. Similarly, intuitives may be drawn to, or distance themselves from, those with a good sensation function, and vice versa. A better understanding of these opposites—latent or dormant in ourselves—can mitigate such reactions, which often have little or nothing to do with the reality of the other person.

To my mind, Jung's model is most helpful when it is used not as a way to classify oneself or others, but rather in the way he originally thought of it, as a psychological compass. So, in any problematic situation, I ask myself four questions:

1) What are the facts? (sensation)
2) Have I thought it through? (thinking)

3) What is it worth to me to pursue this? (feeling)

4) What are the possibilities? (intuition)

The answers aren't always clear, but the questions keep me on my toes. That is by and large why I don't favor type tests. Type tests concretize what is inherently variable, and thereby overlook the dynamic nature of the psyche.

Any system of typology is no more than a gross indicator of what people have in common and the differences between them. Jung's model is no exception. It is distinguished solely by its parameters—the two attitudes and the four functions. What it does not and cannot show, nor does it pretend to, is the uniqueness of the individual. Also, no one is a pure type. It would be foolish to even try to reduce an individual personality to this or that, just one thing or another. Each of us is a conglomeration, an admixture of attitudes and functions that in their combination defy classification. All that is true, and emphatically acknowledged by Jung—

> One can never give a description of a type, no matter how complete, that would apply to more than one individual, despite the fact that in some ways it aptly characterizes thousands of others. Conformity is one side of a man, uniqueness is the other.[83]

—but it does not obviate the practical value of his model, particularly when one has run aground on the shoals of his or her own psychology.

Whether Jung's model is "true" or not—objectively true—is a moot point. Indeed, is anything ever "objectively" true? The real truth is that Jung's model of psychological types has all the advantages and disadvantages of any scientific model. Although lacking statistical verification, it is equally hard to disprove. But it accords with experiential reality. Moreover, since it is based on a fourfold—mandala-like—way of looking at things that is archetypal, it is *psychologically satisfying*. And that's why I favor it.

As mentioned earlier, one's behavior can be quite misleading in determining typology. For instance, to enjoy being with other people is characteristic of the extraverted attitude, but this does not automatically

---

[83] *Psychological Types,* CW 6, par. 895.

92

mean that a person who enjoys lots of company is an extraverted type. Naturally, one's activities will to some extent be determined by typology, but the interpretation of those activities in terms of typology depends on the value system behind the action. Where the subject—oneself—and a personal value system are the dominant motivating factors, there is by definition an introverted type, whether at a party or alone. Similarly, when one is predominantly oriented to the object—things and other people—there is an extraverted type, whether in a crowd or on one's own. This is what makes Jung's system primarily a model of *personality* rather than of behavior.

Everything psychic is relative. I cannot say, think or do anything that is not colored by my particular way of seeing the world, which in turn is a manifestation of both my typology and my complexes. This psychological rule is analogous to Einstein's famous theory of relativity in physics, and equally as significant.

Being aware of the way I tend to function makes it possible for me to assess my attitudes and behavior in a given situation and adjust them accordingly. It enables me both to compensate for my personal disposition and to be tolerant of someone who does not function as I do—someone who has, perhaps, a strength or facility I myself lack.

Typologically speaking, the important question is not whether one is innately inroverted or extraverted, or which function is superior or inferior, but, more pragmatically: in *this* situation, with *that* person, how did I function and with what effect? Did my actions truly reflect my judgments (thinking and feeling) and perceptions (sensation and intuition)? And if not, why not? What complexes were activated in me? To what end? How and why did I mess things up? What does this say about my psychology? What can I do about it? What do I *want* to do about it?

These are among the questions we must take to heart if we want to be psychologically conscious.

****

The Two Attitude Types

According to Jung, his initial motivation for investigating typology was

93

his need to understand why Freud's view of neurosis was so different from that of Adler.

Freud saw his patients as being preeminently dependent upon, and defining themselves in relation to, significant objects, particularly the parents. Adler's emphasis was on how a person, or subject, seeks his own security and supremacy. The one supposes that human behavior is conditioned by the object, the other finds the determining agency in the subject. Jung expressed appreciation for both points of view:

> The Freudian theory is attractively simple, so much so that it almost pains one if anybody drives in the wedge of a contrary assertion. But the same is true of Adler's theory. It too is of illuminating simplicity and explains as much as the Freudian theory. . . . But how comes it that each investigator sees only one side, and why does each maintain that he has the only valid view? . . . Both are obviously working with the same material; but because of personal peculiarities they each see things from a different angle.[84]

Jung concluded that these "personal peculiarities" were in fact due to typological differences: Freud's system was predominantly extraverted, while Adler's was introverted.[85]

These fundamentally opposite attitude types are found in both sexes and at all levels of society. They are not a matter of conscious choice or inheritance or education. Their occurrence is a general phenomenon having an apparently random distribution.

Two children in the same family may even be of opposite types. "Ultimately," writes Jung, "it must be the individual disposition which decides whether [one] will belong to this or that type."[86] In fact, he believed the type antithesis was due to some unconscious, instinctive cause, for which there was likely a biological foundation:

---

[84] *Two Essays,* CW 7, pars. 56f.

[85] Interestingly, Marie-Louise von Franz distinguishes between Freud's psychological system and his personal typology. Freud himself, she believes, was an introverted feeling type, "and therefore his writings bear the characteristics of his inferior extraverted thinking." *(Jung's Typology,* p. 49)

[86] *Psychological Types,* CW 6, par. 560.

There are in nature two fundamentally different modes of adaptation which ensure the continued existence of the living organism. The one consists in a high rate of fertility, with low powers of defence and short duration of life for the single individual; the other consists in equipping the individual with numerous means of self-preservation plus a low fertility rate . . . . [Similarly] the peculiar nature of the extravert constantly urges him to expend and propagate himself in every way, while the tendency of the introvert is to defend himself against all demands from outside, to conserve his energy by withdrawing it from objects, thereby consolidating his own position.[87]

While it is apparent that some individuals have a greater capacity, or disposition, to adapt to life in one way or another, it is not known why. Jung suspected there might be physiological causes of which we have as yet no precise knowledge, since a reversal or distortion of type often proves harmful to one's physical well-being.

No one, of course, is only introverted or extraverted. Although each of us, in the process of following our dominant inclination or adapting to our immediate world, invariably develops one attitude more than the other, the opposite attitude is still potentially there.

Indeed, familial circumstances may force one at an early age to take on an attitude that is not natural, thus violating the individual's innate disposition. "As a rule," writes Jung, "whenever such a falsification of type takes place . . . the individual becomes neurotic later, and can be cured only by developing the attitude consonant with his nature."[88]

This certainly complicates the type issue, since everyone is more or less neurotic—that is, one-sided.

In general, the introvert is simply unconscious of his or her extraverted side, because of an habitual orientation toward the inner world. The extravert's introversion is similarly dormant, waiting to emerge.

In fact, the undeveloped attitude becomes an aspect of the shadow, all those things about ourselves we are not conscious of, our unrealized potential, our unlived life. Moreover, being unconscious, when the inferior

---

[87] Ibid., par. 559.
[88] Ibid., par. 560.

attitude surfaces—that is, when the introvert's extraversion, or the extravert's introversion, is constellated (activated)—it will tend to do so, just like the inferior function, in an emotional, socially unadapted way.

Since what is of value to the introvert is the opposite of what is important to the extravert, the inferior attitude regularly bedevils one's relationships with others.

To illustrate this, Jung tells the story of two youths, one an introverted type, the other extraverted, rambling in the countryside.[89] They come upon a castle. Both want to visit it, but for different reasons. The introvert wonders what it's like inside; the extravert is game for adventure.

At the gate the introvert draws back. "Perhaps we aren't allowed in," he says—imagining guard dogs, policemen and fines in the background. The extravert is undeterred. "Oh, they'll let us in all right," he says—with visions of kindly old watchmen and the possibility of meeting an attractive girl.

On the strength of extraverted optimism, the two finally get inside the castle. There they find some dusty rooms with a collection of old manuscripts. As it happens, old manuscripts are the main interest of the introvert. He whoops with joy and enthusiastically peruses the treasures. He talks to the caretaker, asks for the curator, becomes quite animated; his shyness has vanished, objects have taken on a seductive glamour.

Meanwhile, the spirits of the extravert have fallen. He becomes glum, begins to yawn. There are no kindly watchmen, no pretty girls, just an old castle made into a museum. The manuscripts remind him of a library, library is associated with university, university with studies and examinations. He finds the whole thing incredibly boring.

"Isn't it marvelous," cries the introvert, "look at these!"—to which the extravert replies grumpily, "Nothing here for me, let's go." This annoys the introvert, who secretly swears never again to go rambling with an inconsiderate extravert. The latter is completely frustrated and now can think of nothing but that he'd rather be out of doors on a lovely spring day.

Jung points out that the two youths are wandering together in happy

---

[89] See *Two Essays,* CW 7, pars. 81ff.

symbiosis until they come upon the castle. They enjoy a degree of harmony because they are collectively adapted to each other; the natural attitude of the one complements the natural attitude of the other.

The introvert is curious but hesitant; the extravert opens the door. But once inside, the types invert themselves: the former becomes fascinated by the object, the latter by his negative thoughts. The introvert now cannot be induced to go out and the extravert regrets ever setting foot in the castle.

What has happened? The introvert has become extraverted and the extravert introverted. But the opposite attitude of each manifests in a socially inferior way: the introvert, overpowered by the object, doesn't appreciate that his friend is bored; the extravert, disappointed in his expectations of romantic adventure, becomes moody and sullen, and doesn't care about his friend's excitement.

This is a simple example of the way in which the inferior attitude is autonomous. What we are not conscious of in ourselves is by definition beyond our control. When the undeveloped attitude is constellated, we are prey to all kinds of disruptive emotions—we are "complexed."

In the above story the two youths could be called shadow brothers. In relationships between men and women, the psychological dynamics are better understood through Jung's concept of the contrasexual archetypes: anima—a man's inner ideal image of a woman—and animus—a woman's inner ideal image of a man.[90]

In general, the extraverted man has an introverted anima, while the introverted woman has an extraverted animus, and vice versa. This picture can change through psychological work on oneself, but these inner images are commonly projected onto persons of the opposite sex, with the result that either attitude type is prone to marry its opposite. This is likely to happen because each type is unconsciously complementary to the other.

Recall that the introvert is inclined to be reflective, to think things out and consider carefully before acting. Shyness and a degree of distrust of objects results in hesitation and some difficulty in adapting to the exter-

---

[90] See "The Syzygy: Anima and Animus," *Aion,* CW 9ii.

nal world. The extravert, on the other hand, being attracted to the outer world, is fascinated by new and unknown situations. As a general rule the extravert acts first and thinks afterward; action is swift and not subject to misgivings or hesitation.

"The two types," writes Jung, "therefore seem created for a symbiosis. The one takes care of reflection and the other sees to the initiative and practical action. When the two types marry they may effect an ideal union."[91] Discussing such a typical situation, Jung points out that it is ideal only so long as the partners are occupied with their adaptation to "the manifold external needs of life":

> But when . . . external necessity no longer presses, then they have time to occupy themselves with one another. Hitherto they stood back to back and defended themselves against necessity. But now they turn face to face and look for understanding—only to discover that they have never understood one another. Each speaks a different language. Then the conflict between the two types begins. This struggle is envenomed, brutal, full of mutual depreciation, even when conducted quietly and in the greatest intimacy. For the value of the one is the negation of value for the other.[92]

In the course of life, we are generally obliged to develop both introversion and extraversion to some extent. This is necessary not only in order to coexist with others, but also for the development of individual character. "We cannot in the long run," writes Jung," allow one part of our personality to be cared for symbiotically by another." Yet that is in effect what is happening when we rely on friends, relatives or lovers to carry our inferior attitude or function.

If the inferior attitude is not consciously allowed some expression in our lives, we are likely to become bored and boring, uninteresting to both ourselves and others. And since there is energy tied up with whatever in ourselves is unconscious, we will not have the zest for life that goes with a well-balanced personality.

That's all theory. Now I will tell you of my experience.

---

[91] *Two Essays,* CW 7, par. 80.
[92] Ibid.

19

ARNOLD AND ME

*The superior function is always an expression of the conscious
personality, of its aims, will, and general performance,
whereas the less differentiated functions fall into the category
of things that simply "happen" to one.*[93]

Over the years, Jung's model of typology has been very significant to me
as a psychological compass. But I have to say that I learned almost as
much about typology from living with Arnold as I did from reading Jung.

I met Arnold only a few weeks before leaving for Zurich, where we
had both been accepted to train at the Jung Institute. We took to each
other and agreed to share a place, which I offered to find since I would
be there first. I house-hunted for a week and found a gem.

Arnold, it turned out, was a raving intuitive. I met him at the station
when he arrived. It was the third train I'd met. True to his type, his letter
had been sketchy on details. True to my predominantly sensation orientation, I wasn't.

"I've rented an old house in the country," I told him, hefting his bag.
The lock was broken and the straps were gone. One wheel was missing.
"Twelve and a half minutes on the train and it's never late. The house
has green shutters and polka-dot wallpaper. The garden is bursting with
forsythia, roses, clematis and lily of the valley. The landlady is a Swiss
businesswoman from the Engadine, an attractive blond. She says we can
furnish it the way we want."

"Great!" said Arnold, holding a newspaper over his head. It was pour-
ing rain. He had no hat and he'd forgotten to bring a raincoat. He was
wearing slippers, for God's sake. We couldn't find his trunk because
he'd booked it through to Lucerne.

---

[93] "General Description of the Types," *Psychological Types,* CW 6, par. 575.

99

"Lucerne, Zurich, it's all Switzerland to me," he shrugged.

It was quite amusing at first. I'd never been close to anyone quite so, well, so *different.*

Time meant nothing to Arnold. He missed trains, he missed appointments. He was always late for class, and when he finally found the right room he didn't have anything to write with. He didn't know a budget from a budgie; he either had bags of money or none at all. He didn't know east from west, he got lost whenever he left the house. And sometimes in it.

"You need a seeing-eye dog," I joked.

"Not as long as you're around," he grinned.

He left the stove on overnight. He never turned out lights. Pots boiled over, meat turned black, while he sat on the porch watching the sky and musing. The kitchen was forever filled with the smell of burnt toast. He lost his keys, his wallet, his lecture notes, his passport. He never had a clean shirt. In his old leather jacket, baggy jeans and two different socks he looked like a bum.

His room was always a mess, like a hurricane had hit.

"It drives me crazy just to look at you," I hummed, adjusting my tie in the mirror.

I liked to be neatly turned out, it made me feel good. I knew precisely where everything was. My desk was ordered, my room was always tidy. I turned out the lights when I left the house and I had an excellent sense of direction. I didn't lose anything and I was always on time, or too early. I could cook and I could sew. I knew exactly how much money was in my pocket. Nothing escaped me, I remembered all the details.

"You don't live in the real world," I observed, as Arnold set out to fry an egg. A real hero's journey. He couldn't find the frying pan and when he did he put it on the cold burner.

"Reality as *you* know it," he said, quite hurt.

"Damn!" he cursed. He'd burnt himself again.

I need not say much here about the added aggravations due to Arnold being an extravert and me an introvert. Enough to say there were plenty. He brought people home at all hours of the day and night. I liked privacy, my own quiet space. I was concerned to keep to my timetable. During the day I escaped to my room and studied, or pretended to. At night I lay in bed with a pillow over my head, listening to them carouse.

On the other hand, Arnold's way of functioning was sometimes quite helpful. Like when we furnished the house.

Our landlady, Gretchen, took an immediate fancy to Arnold. God knows why, he didn't present as well as I did. "Just pick out what you want," she said. "You do the shopping, I'll pay the bills."

I had a few things in mind. So did Arnold. My ideas were quite modest, Arnold's were not. We already had beds and a few chairs. "A nice comfortable sofa," I said, as we entered the department store. "A bookcase and a desk for each of us, a couple of lamps. That's all we need."

"You have no imagination," said Arnold, steering me to the antiques. "You do the talking."

Naturally. I had not come to Switzerland without learning some German. Before leaving Canada I took a Berlitz course for six months. I wasn't fluent but I could make myself understood. I could also get by in French. Arnold knew no French and could not even count in German. I think he did not realize he was coming to a foreign country. I scolded him about this more than once.

"A few phrases," I implored. "Try saying hello, *Guten Tag.*"

"Aw," he said, "they all speak English."

As it turned out, they didn't. Worse, and to my chagrin, the language of the streets was Swiss German, a dialect, almost as different from German as Welsh or Scottish is from English. I was just about as helpless as Arnold.

Back to the department store. In one language or another, we managed to spend a lot of our landlady's money. While I fumbled to say exactly what I meant, Arnold waved his hands and gesticulated. By the time we left, ushered out by a grateful crowd of salespeople, we had a few things I hadn't thought of: a Chinese screen, two Indian carpets, a complete set of dishes and cutlery (for eight), ten pounds of bratwurst, a commode reputedly used by Louis XIV, and several numbered prints by Miro and Chagall.

101

Gretchen was thrilled. She gave us a special dinner in her home. Arnold stayed behind when I left. "I'll just wrap up the lease," he winked.

I struggled to appreciate Arnold. I wanted to. His outgoing nature and natural ebullience were charming. I admired his air of careless confidence. He was the life of every party. He easily adapted to new situations. He was a lot more adventurous than me. Where I hung back, tentative and wary, he plowed ahead. He easily made friends. And then brought them home.

He had an uncanny sense of perception. Whenever I got in a rut, bogged down in routine, he had something to suggest. His mind was fertile; it seethed with plans and new ideas. His hunches were usually right. It was like he had a sixth sense, while I was restricted to the usual five. My vision was mundane—where I saw a "thing" or a "person," Arnold saw, well, its soul.

But problems constantly arose between us. When he expressed an intention to do something I took him at his word. I believed he would do what he said he would. This was particularly annoying when we had arranged to meet at a certain time and place and he didn't show up.

"Look," I'd say, "I counted on you being there. I bought the tickets. Where were you?"

"I got waylaid," he'd counter defensively, "something else turned up, I couldn't resist."

"You're unstable, I can't depend on you. You're irresponsible and flighty. Why, you don't have a standpoint at all."

That isn't how Arnold saw it.

"I only express possibilities," he said, when for about the tenth time I accused him of being a social menace. "They aren't real until I say them, and when I do they take on some shape. But that doesn't mean I'll follow up on them. Something better might occur to me. I'm not tied to what I say. I can't help it if you take everything so damned literally."

He went on: "Intuitions are like birds circling in my head. They come and they go. I may not go with them, I never know, but I need time to authenticate their flight."

That was typical. I was prosaic, Arnold was lyrical.

One morning I got up to find yet another pot boiled empty on a hot burner. Arnold struggled out of bed, looking for his glasses.

"Have you seen my razor?" he called.

"God damn it!" I shouted, furious, grabbing an oven mitt, "one day you'll burn down the house, we'll both be cinders. 'Alas,' they'll say, scooping our remains into little jars to send back to our loved ones, 'they had such potential. Too bad one of them was such a klutz!' "

Arnold shuffled into the kitchen as I threw the pot out the door.

"Oh yeah?" he said. "You made dinner last night for Cynthia, I wasn't even here."

It was true. My face got red. My balloon had been pricked. Reality as I knew it just got bigger.

"I forgot," I said meekly.

Arnold clapped his hands and danced around the room. "Join the human race!" he sang. As usual, he couldn't hold a note.

Only then did I realize that Arnold was my shadow. This was a revelation. It shouldn't have been, since we had already established that our complexes were radically different, but it struck me like a thunderbolt. I said as much to Arnold.

"You goof," he said. "You're my shadow as well. That's why you drive me up the wall."

We embraced.

All that was a long time ago. In the intervening years I've become more like Arnold. And he, more like me. Not only can he tell left from right now, he irons his tee-shirts and has learned to crochet. He dresses impeccably and his attention to detail is often sharper than mine. He lives alone and has a fabulous garden. He knows the names of all the flowers, in Latin.

Meanwhile, I have dinner parties and have been known to haunt the bars till dawn. I misplace precious papers. I forget names and telephone numbers. I can no longer find my way around a strange city. I pursue possibilities while things-to-do pile up around me. I could not cope without a cleaning lady.

Such developments are the unexpected consequences of getting to know your shadow and incorporating it in your life. You lose something of what you were, but you add a dimension that wasn't there before. Where you were one-sided, you find a balance. You learn to appreciate those who function differently and you develop a new attitude toward yourself.

Arnold and I are still shadow brothers, but now the tables are turned.

I tell him about my latest escapade. He shakes his head. "You damn gadabout," he says, punching my shoulder.

Arnold describes quiet evenings by the fire with a few intimate friends and says he never wants to travel again. This man, this great oaf, who used to be off and running at the drop of a hat.

"You're dull and predictable," I remark, cuffing him.

When Arnold died some twenty years ago, I cried for a week.

20

THE COMPLEXITY OF LIFE

Everyone knows nowadays that people "have complexes."
What is not so well known, though far more important theoretically, is that
complexes can have us.[94]

We like to think we are masters in our own house, but clearly we are not. We are renters at best. Psychologically we live in a boarding house of saints and knaves, nobles and villains, run by a landlord who for all we know is indifferent to the lot. We fancy we can do what we want, but when it comes to a showdown our will is hampered by fellow boarders with a mind of their own.

In the jargon of Jungian psychology, these "fellow boarders" are known as complexes.

Just as atoms and molecules are the invisible components of physical objects, complexes are the building blocks of the psyche. Complexes in themselves are not negative, but their effects often are, for they determine our emotional reactions.

When I first went into analysis I knew nothing about complexes. I knew only that I was at the end of my rope, on my knees. Then I took Jung's Word Association Experiment, a test he developed almost a century ago to illustrate how unconscious factors can disturb the workings of consciousness. It is the precursor of the modern lie detector test, though rather more revealing in its broader scope.

In the Word Association Experiment an examiner reads from a list of a hundred words, to each of which you are asked to respond with what first comes into your head. The delay in responding (the response time)

---

[94] "A Review of the Complex Theory," *The Structure and Dynamics of the Psyche,* CW 8, par. 200.

is measured with a stop watch.

Here is how it goes:

"Head"— "bed" (0.8 sec.)
"Marry"— "together" (1.7 sec.)
"Woman"— "friend" (2 sec.)
"Home"—(long pause) "none" (5.6 sec.)

—and so on.

Then the examiner takes you through the list a second time, noting different responses to the same words. Finally you are asked for comments on those words to which you had a longer-than-average response time, a merely mechanical response or a different association on the second run-through. All these had been flagged by the examiner as "complex indicators."

My experience of the Word Association Experiment was both illuminating and deflating. It convinced me that complexes were not only real but were alive in me and quite autonomous, independent of my will. I realized they could affect my memory, my thoughts, my moods, my behavior. I was not free to be me—there *was* no "me"—when I was in the grip of a complex.

Freud described dreams as the *via regia* to the unconscious; Jung showed that the royal road to the unconscious is rather the complex, the architect of both dreams and symptoms. In fact, Jung originally gave the name "complex psychology" to his school of thought, to distinguish it from Freud's school of psychoanalysis.

The activation of a complex is always marked by the presence of some strong emotion, be it love or hate, joy or anger, or any other. We are all complexed by something, which is to say, we all react emotionally when the right buttons are pushed. Or, to put it another way, an emotional reaction *means* that a complex has been constellated. When a complex is activated we can't think straight and hardly know how we feel. We speak and act according to the dictates of the complex, and when it has run its course we wonder what took over.

We cannot get rid of our complexes, simply because they are deeply rooted in our personal history. Complexes are part and parcel of who we are. The most we can do is become aware of how we are influenced by them and how they interfere with our conscious intentions. As long as we are unconscious of our complexes, we are prone to being overwhelmed or driven by them. When we understand them, they lose their power to affect us. They do not disappear, but over time their grip on us can loosen.

A complex is a bundle of associations, sometimes painful, sometimes joyful, always accompanied by affect. It has energy and a life of its own. It can upset digestion, breathing and the rate at which the heart beats. It behaves like a partial personality. When we want to say or do something and a complex interferes, we find ourselves saying or doing something quite different from what we intended. Our best intentions are upset, exactly as if we had been interfered with by another person.

Complexes can take over to such an extent that they become visible and audible. They appear as visions and speak in voices that are like those of definite people. This is not necessarily a pathological symptom (e.g., schizophrenia). Complexes are regularly personified in dreams, and one can train oneself so they become visible or audible also in a waking condition, as in the practice of active imagination.[95] It is even psychologically healthy to do so, for when you give them a voice, a face, a personality, they are less likely to take over when you're not looking.

The existence of complexes goes a long way toward explaining both multiple personality disorders and what the helping professions call lost memory recovery. An early trauma is often at the root of such cases. What may happen in response to a painful traumatic event is that the ego dissociates. The self-regulating function of the psyche is activated and creates a complex that dis-remembers the event—it gets buried among the detritus of ongoing life.[96] Like any other complex, it lies dogg-o in the unconscious until something happens to trigger it.

Over the past hundred years the word "complex" has become common currency, but what it means, and the effects complexes have on our lives,

---

[95] See below, pp. 106ff.

[96] See above, pp. 55ff., for commentary on the self-regulating function of the psyche, a keynote belief in the practice of Jungian analysis.

are not so widely understood. This is unfortunate, for until we realize that, as Jung says, "complexes can have us," we are doomed to live a life forever hampered by them, forever ruled by inner forces, forever at odds with others.

And don't forget the difference between a fact (e.g., "Politicians often wear suits") and an opinion (e.g., "Among politicians, brains are as rare as fur on fish"). Invariably, opinions derive from complexes. Not my fault, just the messenger.

****

This is choice and I can't resist quoting it:

> She writes like a middle-aged French *roué*. She writes like Carl Jung dreaming he is Candide.
> —*John Barth* on Susan Sontag.[97]

---

[97] Jon Winokur, ed. *W.O.W.: Writers on Writing,* p. 86 (*roué* = rake, trickster).

21

WHO ARE WE, REALLY?

*The persona is that which in reality one is not,
but which oneself as well as others think one is.*[98]

We have a name, perhaps a title, perform a function in the outside world. We are this, that or the other. To some extent all this is real, yet in relation to our essential individuality, what we seem to be is only a secondary, superficial reality.

Jung describes the persona as an aspect of the collective psyche, which means there is nothing individual about it. It may *feel* individual—quite special and unique, in fact—but our persona is on the one hand simply a social identity, and on the other an ideal image of ourselves.

Like any other complex, one's persona has certain attributes and behavior patterns associated with it, as well as collective expectations to live up to: a struggling writer, for instance, is a serious thinker, on the brink of recognition; a teacher is a figure of authority, dedicated to imparting knowledge; a doctor is wise, versed in the arcane mysteries of the body; a priest is close to God, morally impeccable; a mother loves her children and would sacrifice her life for them; an accountant knows his figures but is unemotional, and so on.

That is why we experience a sense of shock when we read of a teacher accused of molesting a student; a doctor charged with drug abuse; a priest on the hook for pedophilia; a mother who breaks her children's bones, or kills them; an accountant who fiddles the books; a pillar of the community caught with his pants down.

The development of a collectively suitable persona always involves a compromise between what we know ourselves to be and what is ex-

---

[98] "Concerning Rebirth," *The Archetypes and the Collective Unconscious,* CW 9i, par. 221.

pected of us, such as a degree of courtesy and innocuous behavior. There is nothing intrinsically wrong with that. In Greek, the word *persona* meant a mask worn by actors to indicate the role they played. On this level, it is an asset in mixing with other people. It is also useful as a protective covering. Close friends may know us for what we are; the rest of the world knows only what we choose to show them. Indeed, without an outer layer of some kind, we are simply too vulnerable. Only the foolish and naive attempt to move through life without a persona.

However, we must be able to drop our persona in situations where it is not appropriate. This is especially true in intimate relationships. There is a difference between myself as an analyst and who I am when I'm not practicing. The doctor's professional bedside manner is little comfort to a neglected mate. The teacher's credentials do not impress her teenage son who wants to borrow the car. The wise preacher leaves his collar and his rhetoric at home when he goes courting.

By handsomely rewarding the persona, the outside world invites us to identify with it. Money, respect and power come to those who can perform single-mindedly and well in a social role. No wonder we can forget that our essential identity is something other than the work we do, our function in the collective. From being a useful convenience, therefore, the persona easily becomes a trap. It is one thing to realize this, but quite another to do something about it.

The poet Rainer Maria Rilke put it quite well:

We discover, indeed, that we do not know our part; we look for a mirror; we want to rub off the paint, to remove all that is artificial and become real. But somewhere a bit of mummery that we forget still sticks to us. A trace of exaggeration remains in our eyebrows; we do not notice that the corners of our lips are twisted. And thus we go about, a laughing-stock, a mere half-thing: neither real beings nor actors.[99]

Identification with a social role is a frequent source of midlife crisis. This is so because it inhibits our adaptation to a given situation beyond what is collectively prescribed. Who am I without a mask? Is there any-

---

[99] *The Notebook of Malte Laurids Brigge*, p. 217.

body home? I am a prominent and respected member of the community. Why, then, is my wife interested in someone else?

Many married people cultivate a joint persona as "a happy couple." Whatever may be happening between them, they greet the world with a united front. They are perfectly matched, the envy of their friends. What goes on behind the curtains is anybody's guess, and nobody's else's business, for sure, but how many "happy couples" feel trapped in their persona and stay together simply because they don't know who they are otherwise?

We cannot get rid of ourselves in favor of a collective identity without some consequences. We lose sight of who we are without our protective covering; our reactions are predetermined by collective expectations (we do and think and feel what our persona "should" do, think and feel); erratic moods betray our real feelings; those close to us complain of our emotional distance; and, worst of all, we cannot imagine life without our persona.

Assuming we recognize the problem, and suffer because of it, what are we to do about it? Personal analysis is a possibility for those who have the time and can afford it. Otherwise, some reading in the literature of depth psychology would not go amiss. But avoid "motivational speakers" and "quick-fix" books, confessional memoirs by those who would seduce you into imitating them. Your task is to discover who *you* are.

Here are some tips:

1) Pay attention to your dreams; mull over their content, and don't think you have to "understand" them to get the message.

2) Monitor your feelings in both intimate and social situations.

3) Become aware of how and when you use your persona for legitimate reasons, and when you are simply hiding behind it.

4) Think about what it means to lead an authentic life.

22

TWELVE BELLS
& THE RAZR'S EDGE

Shit, midnight already, and I haven't even started writing.

I would be glad to have a mate, but I have wondered lately what I have to offer a woman, except a lustful appetite and a desire for a relationship based on a degree of intimacy that involves considerable psychological awareness. Is this enough, or too much to ask? I flounder and twist myself into knots in my turret, or call it a badger's sett, why not?

Let me give this over to Razr, who has a tale to tell.

****

"This isn't what I expected," said Annabelle, sitting precariously on the edge of my bed. She had showered and now looked quite presentable. She wore one of my smallest t-shirts and her own pink panties.

She was petite, thirty-something, and quite pretty without the punk make-up. I had found her hiding in a corner of my local pub and enticed her to follow me home. It wasn't lust. I was just feeling lonely and wanted someone to talk to. My mistake. Annabelle wasn't exactly an airhead, but conversation was not her strong suit. She had street smarts and may have scraped through Grade Eight. I liked her.

Annabelle curled up, disconcerted. "Don't you want to, you know, fool around?" she asked.

I stood my ground, fully dressed. "I would like to get to know you."

Annabelle hung her head, tearful. "Mr. Razr, I am a nobody. I ran away from an orphanage years ago, and there is no one who cares for me. I live on the street."

My heart was wrenched. "How do you buy vegetables?"

"I give men sex," said Annabelle. "They give me a bunch of dollars and walk away. I don't feel good about myself, and I bin so lonely."

Oh Jeez, what to say and what to do?

"Baby, you can drive my car," I smiled. And so did she.

I tucked her in and went upstairs to the guest bedroom, bemused.

23
BUCKET'S FULL

Well, I don't relish leaving you there, hanging out on a limb, wondering what foolishness I might come up with next.

Case in point: Whatever became of Ms. Bo Peep? Well, she did come to visit and stayed a few weeks in the ensuiteheart I created for her. She was affectionate but understandably reticent for a week, groggy from jet-lag. "I have a husband and little ones in the Alps to think about," she explained. But one day she woke up bright-eyed and bushy-tailed.

"What is your pleasure today?" she asked.

"My wish, sweetheart, is that you would be overcome with the desire to constellate my inner Razr."

"I'll get back to you on that," she smiled.

We did subsequently bond, she shy but forthcoming. I do love her.

****

So with that, I'm plumb wrote out. Well, for the time being, anyway. I 'spect I'll be back again before too long, for I have miles to go before I sleep, and many more tears to weep.

> We shall not cease from exploration
> And the end of all our exploring
> Will be to arrive where we started
> And know the place for the first time.[100]

****

And finally, again, my beloved Emerson:

> Trust thyself: every heart vibrates to that iron string. Accept the place the divine providence has found for you, the society of your contemporaries, the connection of events. Great men have always done so.[101]

---

[100] T. S. Eliot, "Little Gidding," in *Four Quartets,* p. 59.
[101] "Self-Reliance," in *Essays: First and Second Series,* p. 30.

BIBLIOGRAPHY
(including recommended reading)

Carmichael, Hoagland. *The Stardust Road & Sometimes I Wonder: The Autobi-ographies of Hoagy Carmichael.* Intro. John Edward Hasse. New York: Da Capo Press, 1999.

Carotenuto, Aldo. *Eros and Pathos: Shades of Love and Suffering.* Toronto: Inner City Books, 1989.

Cohen, Leonard. *Book of Longing.* Toronto: McClelland & Stewart Ltd., 2006.

Daumal, René. *Mount Analogue: An Authentic Narrative.* Trans. and Intro. Robert Shattuck. London, UK: Vincent Stuart Publishers Ltd., 1959.

De Vries, Ad. *Dictionary of Symbols and Imagery.* Amsterdam: North-Holland Publishing Company, 1976.

Edinger, Edward F. *Anatomy of the Psyche: Alchemical Symbolism in Psycho-therapy.* La Salle, IL: Open Court, 1985.

_____. *The Creation of Consciousness: Jung's Myth for Modern Man.* Toronto: Inner City Books, 1984.

_____. "M. Esther Harding, 1888-1971." In *Spring 1972.* Zurich: Spring Publications, 1972.

_____. *The Mysterium Lectures: A Journey Through Jung's* Mysterium Coniunctionis. Toronto: Inner City Books, 1995.

_____. *The Mystery of the Coniunctio: Alchemical Image of Individuation.* Toronto: Inner City Books, 1994.

_____. *Transformation of the God-Image: An Elucidation of Jung's* Answer to Job. Toronto: Inner City Books, 1992.

_____. *Science of the Soul: A Jungian Perspective.* Toronto: Inner City Books, 2002.

Elder, George R., and Cordic, Dianne D., eds. *An American Jungian: In Honor of Edward F. Edinger.* Toronto: Inner City Books, 2009.

Eliot, T. S. *Four Quartets.* London, UK: Faber and Faber Limited, 1959.

Emerson, Ralph Waldo. *Essays: First and Second Series.* Intr. Douglas Crase. New York: Penguin Books (Library of America), 2010.

_____. *Selected Journals, 1841-1877*. New York: Penguin Books (Library of America), 2010.

Frey-Rohn, Liliane. *From Freud to Jung: A Comparative Study of the Psychology of the Unconscious*. Boston: Shambhala Publications, 1974.

Frost, Robert. "Stopping by Woods on a Snowy Evening." In "The Poetry of Robert Frost," Ed. Edward Connery Lathem, from *The Random House Book of Poetry for Children*. New York: Random House, 1983.

Grimm Brothers. *The Complete Grimm's Fairy Tales*. New York: Pantheon Books, 1944.

Hall, James A., and Sharp, Daryl, eds. *Marie-Louise von Franz: The Classic Jungian and the Classic Jungian Tradition*. Toronto: Inner City Books, 2008.

Hannah, Barbara. *Jung: His Life and Work (A Biographical Memoir)*. New York: Capricorn Books, G.P. Putnam's Sons, 1976.

Hillenbrand, Laura. *Seabiscuit: An American Legend*. New York: Random House, 2001.

Hollis, James. *The Middle Passage: From Misery to Meaning in Midlife*. Toronto: Inner City Books, 1993.

_____. *The Eden Project: In Search of the Magical Other*. Toronto: Inner City Books, 1998.

_____. *Under Saturn's Shadow: The Wounding and Healing of Men*. Toronto: Inner City Books, 1994.

Jacoby, Mario. *The Analytic Encounter: Transference and Human Relationship*. Toronto: Inner City Books, 1984.

_____. *Longing for Paradise: Psychological Perspectives on an Archetype*. Toronto: Inner City Books, 2006.

Jung, C. G. *C. G. Jung Letters*. (Bollingen Series XCV). 2 vols. Ed. G. Adler and A. Jaffé. Princeton: Princeton University Press, 1973.

_____. *The Collected Works of C. G. Jung* (Bollingen Series XX). 20 vols. Trans. R. F. C. Hull. Ed. H. Read, M. Fordham, G. Adler, Wm. McGuire. Princeton: Princeton University Press, 1953-1979.

_____. *Memories, Dreams, Reflections*. Ed. Aniela Jaffé. New York: Pantheon Books, 1961.

_____. *The Psychology of Kundalini Yoga: Notes of the Seminar Given in*

1932 by C.G. Jung (Bollingen Series XCIX). Ed. Sonu Shamdasani. Princeton: Princeton University Press, 1996.

_____. *Visions: Notes of the Seminar Given in 1930-1934* (Bollingen Series XCIX). 2 vols. Ed. Claire Douglas. Princeton: Princeton University Press, 1997.

Jung, Carl G., and von Franz, Marie-Louise, eds. *Man and His Symbols*. London, UK: Aldus Books, 1964.

Kacirk, Jeffrey. *Jeffrey Kacirk's Forgotten English: A 365-Day Calendar of Vanishing Vocabulary and Folklore for 2011*. Petaluma, CA: Pomegranate Communications, Inc., 2010.

Kafka, Franz. *The Diaries of Franz Kafka, 1910-1913*. Trans. Joseph Kresh. Ed. Max Brod. London: Secker & Warburg, 1948.

_____. *The Diaries of Franz Kafka, 1914-1923*. Trans. Martin Greenberg. Ed. Max Brod. London: Secker & Warburg, 1949.

_____. *The Great Wall of China and Other Pieces*. Trans. Willa and Edwin Muir. London: Secker & Warburg, 1946.

Kaufmann, Walter, ed. and trans. *The Portable Nietzsche*. New York: Viking Press, 1954.

Kierkegaard, Søren. *The Journals of Kierkegaard: 1834-1854*. Ed. and trans. Alexander Dru. Oxford, UK: Oxford University Press, 1958.

Luton, Frith. *Bees, Honey and the Hive: Circumambulating the Centre (A Jungian Exploration of the Symbolism and Psychology)*. Toronto: Inner City Books, 2011.

Malcolm, Janet. *Psychoanalysis: The Impossible Profession*. New York: Alfred A. Knopf, 1981.

McGuire, William, ed. *The Freud/Jung Letters* (Bollingen Series XCIV). Trans. Ralph Manheim and R. F. C. Hull. Princeton: Princeton University Press, 1974.

McGuire, William, and Hull, R. F. C., eds. *C. G. Jung Speaking: Interviews and Encounters* (Bollingen Series XCVII). Princeton: Princeton University Press, 1977.

Meredith, Margaret Eileen. *The Secret Garden: Temenos for Individuation*. Toronto: Inner City Books, 2005.

Miller, Henry. *The Wisdom of the Heart*. New York: New Directions, 1950.

116

Monick, Eugene. *Phallos: Sacred Image of the Masculine.* Toronto: Inner City Books, 1987.

Perera, Sylvia Brinton. *Descent to the Goddess: A Way of Initiation for Women.* Toronto: Inner City Books, 1981.

_____. *The Scapegoat Complex: Toward a Mythology of Shadow and Guilt.* Toronto: Inner City Books, 1986.

Plato. *The Dialogues of Plato.* New York: Random House, 1965.

Qualls-Corbett, Nancy. *The Sacred Prostitute: Eternal Aspect of the Feminine.* Toronto: Inner City Books, 1988.

Rank, Otto. *The Trauma of Birth.* New York: Brunner, 1952.

Rilke, Rainer Maria. *The Notebook of Malte Laurids Brigge.* Trans. John Linton. London, UK: The Hogarth Press, 1959.

_____. *Rilke on Love and Other Difficulties.* Ed. John Mood. New York, Norton, 1975.

_____. *Rainer Maria Rilke, Sonnets to Orpheus.* Trans. Willis Barnstone. Boston, MA: Shambhala, 2004.

Sharp, Daryl. *The Brillig Trilogy.* See below: *Chicken Little; Who Am I, Really?; and Living Jung.*

_____. *Chicken Little: The Inside Story (a Jungian romance).* Toronto: Inner City Books, 1993.

_____. *C. G. Jung Lexicon: A Primer of Terms and Concepts.* Toronto: Inner City Books, 1991.

_____. *Dear Gladys: The Survival Papers, Book 2.* Toronto: Inner City Books, 1989.

_____. *Digesting Jung: Food for the Journey.* Toronto: Inner City Books, 2001.

_____. *Eyes Wide Open: Late Thoughts (a Jungian romance).* Toronto: Inner City Books, 2007.

_____. *Getting To Know You: The Inside Out of Relationship.* Toronto: Inner City Books, 1992.

_____. *Jung Uncorked: Rare Vintages from the Cellar of Analytical Psychology.* 4 vols. Toronto: Inner City Books, 2008-9.

_____. *Jungian Psychology Unplugged: My Life as an Elephant.* Toronto, Inner City Books, 1998.

_____. *Live Your Nonsense: Halfway to Dawn with Eros (A Jungian Perspective on Individuation).* Toronto: Inner City Books, 2010.

_____. *Living Jung: The Good and the Better.* Toronto: Inner City Books, 1966.

_____. *Not the Big Sleep: On Having Fun, Seriously (a Jungian romance).* Toronto: Inner City Books, 2005.

_____. *On Staying Awake: Getting Older and Bolder (another Jungian romance).* Toronto: Inner City Books, 2006.

_____. *Personality Types: Jung's Model of Typology.* Toronto: Inner City Books, 1987.

_____. *The Eros Trilogy.* See *Live Your Nonsense, Trampled to Death by Geese,* and *Hijacked by Eros.*

_____. *The Secret Raven: Conflict and Transformation in the Life of Franz Kafka.* Toronto: Inner City Books, 1980.

_____. *The Survival Papers: Anatomy of a Midlife Crisis.* Toronto: Inner City Books, 1988.

_____. *Trampled to Death by Geese: More Eros, and a Lot More Nonsense (A Jungian analyst's whimsical perspective on the Inner Life).* Toronto: Inner City Books, 2011.

_____. *Who Am I, Really? Personality, Soul and Individuation.* Toronto: Inner City Books, 1995.

Sparks, J. Gary. *At the Heart of Matter: Synchronicity and Jung's Spiritual Testament.* Toronto: Inner City Books, 2007.

_____. *In the Valley of Diamonds: Adventures in* Number and Time *with Marie-Louise von Franz.* Toronto: Inner City Books, 2009.

Stein, Gertrude. *Geography and Plays.* New York: Random House, 1922.

Steinberg, Warren. *Circle of Care: Clinical Issues in Jungian Therapy.* Toronto: Inner City Books, 1990.

Stevens, Anthony. *Archetype Revisited: An Updated Natural History of the Self.* Toronto: Inner City Books, 2003.

Storr, Anthony. *Solitude.* London, UK: HarperCollins Publishers, 1997.

Thomas, Dylan. *Dylan Thomas: Collected Poems, 1934-1952.* London, UK: Aldine Press for J .M. Dent & Sons Ltd., 1971.

Von Franz, Marie-Louise. *Alchemy: An Introduction to the Symbolism and the Psychology.* Toronto: Inner City Books, 1980.

_____. *Animus and Anima in Fairy Tales.* Toronto: Inner City Books, 2002.

_____. *Archetypal Dimensions of the Psyche.* Boston: Shambhala Publications, 1997.

_____. *C. G. Jung: His Myth in Our Time.* Toronto: Inner City Books, 1998.

_____. *Individuation in Fairy Tales.* Zurich: Spring Publications, 1977.

_____. *On Divination and Synchronicity.* Toronto: Inner City Books, 1980.

_____. *On Dreams and Death: A Jungian Interpretation.* Foreword by Emmanuel Kennedy-Xipolitas, Trans. Emmanuel Kennedy-Xipolitas and Vernon Brooks. Chicago, IL: Open Court, 1998.

_____. *The Problem of the Puer Aeternus.* Revised edition. Ed. Daryl Sharp. Toronto: Inner City Books, 2000.

_____. *Projection and Re-Collection in Jungian Psychology: Reflections of the Soul.* Trans. William H. Kennedy. La Salle, IL: Open Court, 1980.

_____. *Redemption Motifs in Fairy Tales.* Toronto: Inner City Books, 1980.

Von Franz, Marie-Louise, and Hillman, James. *Jung's Typology.* New York: Spring Publications, 1971.

Wilhelm, Richard, trans. *The I Ching or Book of Changes.* Rendered into English by Cary F. Baynes. London, UK: Routledge & Kegan Paul, 1968.

Winokur, Jon, ed. *W.O.W.: Writers on Writing.* Philadelphia, PA: Running Press, 1990.

Yeoman, Ann. *Now or Neverland: Peter Pan and the Myth of Eternal Youth.* Toronto: Inner City Books, 1999.

Index

Virgin Mary, 45-46
von Franz, Marie-Louise: 14-15
  Individuation in Fairy Tales, 19
  The Problem of the Puer Aeternus,
    14-15
  on typology, 94n

Washington, Dinah, 43
waterfall, 81
Waters, Muddy, 16, 69
Weinstein, Harvey: *My Life with Marilyn,* 30-31
welcome wagon, 23
wholeness, 62-64, 76-77
Williams, Michelle, 30
Winokur, Jon: W.O.W.: *Writers on*

Writing, 108
Wisdom, 43. *See also* Sophia
women, as sex objects, 18-19, 28-29
Woolf, Toni, 61

Word Association Experiment, 105-106
"working on oneself", 38-39
writing, 47, 48, 85-86

Yeoman, Ann: *Now or Neverland,* 14n
yin/yang, 47
Young, Neil, 16
Yusuf Islam, 79. *See also* Cat Stevens

Zeus, 62-64, 76

Also in this Series by Daryl Sharp

Please see next page for discounts and postage/handling.

THE SECRET RAVEN
Conflict and Transformation in the Life of Franz Kafka
ISBN 978-0-919123-00-7. (1980) 128 pp. $25

PERSONALITY TYPES: Jung's Model of Typology
ISBN 978-0-919123-30-9. (1987) 128 pp. **Diagrams** $25

THE SURVIVAL PAPERS: Anatomy of a Midlife Crisis
ISBN 978-0-919123-34-2. (1988) 160 pp. $25

DEAR GLADYS: The Survival Papers, Book 2
ISBN 978-0-919123-36-6. (1989) 144 pp. $25

JUNG LEXICON: A Primer of Terms and Concepts
ISBN 978-0-919123-48-9. (1991) 160 pp. **Diagrams** $25

GETTING TO KNOW YOU: The Inside Out of Relationship
ISBN 978-0-919123-56-4. (1992) 128 pp. $25

THE BRILLIG TRILOGY:

1. CHICKEN LITTLE: The Inside Story *(A Jungian romance)*
ISBN 978-0-919123-62-5. (1993) 128 pp. $25

2. WHO AM I, REALLY? Personality, Soul and Individuation
ISBN 978-0-919123-68-7. (1995) 144 pp. $25

3. LIVING JUNG: The Good and the Better
ISBN 978-0-919123-73-1. (1996) 128 pp. $25

JUNGIAN PSYCHOLOGY UNPLUGGED: My Life as an Elephant
ISBN 978-0-919123-81-6. (1998) 160 pp. $25

DIGESTING JUNG: Food for the Journey
ISBN 978-0-919123-96-0. (2001) 128 pp. $25

JUNG UNCORKED: Rare Vintages from the Cellar of Analytical Psychology
Three books. ISBN 978-1-894574-21-1/22-8/24-2 (2008-9) 128 pp. each. $25 each

THE SLEEPNOT TRILOGY:

1. NOT THE BIG SLEEP: On having fun, seriously *(A Jungian romance)*
ISBN 978-0-894574-13-6. (2005) 128 pp. $25

2. ON STAYING AWAKE: Getting Older and Bolder *(Another Jungian romance)*
ISBN 978-0-894574-16-7. (2006) 144 pp. $25

3. EYES WIDE OPEN: Late Thoughts *(Another Jungian romance)*
ISBN 978-0-894574-18-1. (2007) 160 pp. $25

Studies in Jungian Psychology
by Jungian Analysts

Quality Paperbacks

Prices and payment in $US (except in Canada and Visa orders, $Cdn)

Bees, Honey and the Hive: Circumambulating the Centre.
Frith Luton (Melbourne) ISBN 978-1-894574-32-7. 208 pp. $30

Risky Business: Environmental Disasters and the Nature Archetype
Stephen Foster (Boulder, CO) ISBN 978-0-919123-33-4. 128 pp. $25

Miles To Go Before I Sleep: Growing Up Puer (a Jungian Romance)
Daryl Sharp (Toronto) 978-1-894574-36-5 128 pp. $25

Conscious Femininity: Interviews with Marion Woodman
Introduction by Marion Woodman (Toronto) ISBN 978-0-919123-59-5. 160 pp. $25

The Sacred Psyche: A Psychological Approach to the Psalms
Edward F. Edinger (Los Angeles) ISBN 978-1-894574-09-9. 160 pp. $25

Eros and Pathos: Shades of Love and Suffering
Aldo Carotenuto (Rome) ISBN 978- 0-919123-39-7. 144 pp. $25

Descent to the Goddess: A Way of Initiation for Women
Sylvia Brinton Perera (New York) ISBN 978-0-919123-05-2. 112 pp. $25

The Illness That We Are: A Jungian Critique of Christianity
John P. Dourley (Ottawa) ISBN 978-0-919123-16-8. 128 pp. $25

Coming To Age: The Croning Years and Late-Life Transformation
Jane R. Prétat (Providence) ISBN 978-0-919123-63-2. 144 pp. $25

Jungian Dream Interpretation: A Handbook of Theory and Practice
James A. Hall, M.D. (Dallas) ISBN 978-0-919123-12-0. 128 pp. $25

Phallos: Sacred Image of the Masculine
Eugene Monick (Scranton) ISBN 978-0-919123-26-7. 30 illustrations. 144 pp. $25

The Sacred Prostitute: Eternal Aspect of the Feminine
Nancy Qualls-Corbett (Birmingham) ISBN 978-0-919123-31-1. Illustrated. 176 pp. $30

Jung Uncorked: Rare Vintages from the Cellar of Analytical Psychology
Three vols. Daryl Sharp (Toronto) ISBN 978-1-894574-21-1/22-8/24-2. 128 pp. $25 each

The Pregnant Virgin: A Process of Psychological Development
Marion Woodman (Toronto) ISBN 978-0-919123-20-5. Illustrated. 208 pp. $30pb/$35hc

Discounts: any 3-5 books, 10%; 6-9 books, 20%; 10-19, 25%; 20 or more, 40% .

Add Postage/Handling: 1-2 books, $6 surface ($10 air); 3-4 books, $12 surface ($16 air); 5-9 books, $16 surface ($25 air); 10 or more, $16 surface ($30 air)

Visa credit cards accepted. Toll-free: Tel. 1-888-927-0355; Fax 1-888=924-1814.

INNER CITY BOOKS, Box 1271, Station Q, Toronto, ON M4T 2P4, Canada
Tel. (416) 927-0355 / Fax (416) 924-1814 / booksales@innercitybooks.net